T0370514

Customizable Agile Development

Crafting Innovative Agile Frameworks to Suit Your Business Needs

Kanika Sud

Apress®

Customizable Agile Development: Crafting Innovative Agile Frameworks to Suit Your Business Needs

Kanika Sud
Shimla, Himachal Pradesh, India

ISBN-13 (pbk): 979-8-8688-1054-1   ISBN-13 (electronic): 979-8-8688-1055-8
https://doi.org/10.1007/979-8-8688-1055-8

Copyright © 2025 by Kanika Sud

This work is subject to copyright. All rights are reserved by the Publisher, whether the whole or part of the material is concerned, specifically the rights of translation, reprinting, reuse of illustrations, recitation, broadcasting, reproduction on microfilms or in any other physical way, and transmission or information storage and retrieval, electronic adaptation, computer software, or by similar or dissimilar methodology now known or hereafter developed.

Trademarked names, logos, and images may appear in this book. Rather than use a trademark symbol with every occurrence of a trademarked name, logo, or image we use the names, logos, and images only in an editorial fashion and to the benefit of the trademark owner, with no intention of infringement of the trademark.

The use in this publication of trade names, trademarks, service marks, and similar terms, even if they are not identified as such, is not to be taken as an expression of opinion as to whether or not they are subject to proprietary rights.

While the advice and information in this book are believed to be true and accurate at the date of publication, neither the authors nor the editors nor the publisher can accept any legal responsibility for any errors or omissions that may be made. The publisher makes no warranty, express or implied, with respect to the material contained herein.

Managing Director, Apress Media LLC: Welmoed Spahr
Acquisitions Editor: James Robinson-Prior
Development Editor: James Markham
Editorial Assistant: Gryffin Winkler

Cover designed by eStudioCalamar

Distributed to the book trade worldwide by Springer Science+Business Media New York, 1 New York Plaza, Suite 4600, New York, NY 10004-1562, USA. Phone 1-800-SPRINGER, fax (201) 348-4505, e-mail orders-ny@springer-sbm.com, or visit www.springeronline.com. Apress Media, LLC is a California LLC and the sole member (owner) is Springer Science + Business Media Finance Inc (SSBM Finance Inc). SSBM Finance Inc is a **Delaware** corporation.

For information on translations, please e-mail booktranslations@springernature.com; for reprint, paperback, or audio rights, please e-mail bookpermissions@springernature.com.

Apress titles may be purchased in bulk for academic, corporate, or promotional use. eBook versions and licenses are also available for most titles. For more information, reference our Print and eBook Bulk Sales web page at http://www.apress.com/bulk-sales.

Any source code or other supplementary material referenced by the author in this book is available to readers on GitHub. For more detailed information, please visit https://www.apress.com/gp/services/source-code.

If disposing of this product, please recycle the paper

Table of Contents

About the Author

 **Kanika Sud** is a professionally certified product owner who loves shaping solutions through design thinking and business storytelling. Kanika has been part of the tech industry for around 14 years, with a holistic experience of management and design thinking, entrepreneurship, front-end and back-end software development, and quality assurance.

About the Technical Reviewer

 **Eldon Alameda** is a seasoned technical leader, author, and software innovator with over two decades of experience in agile development, architecture design, and full-stack programming. As the author of two Ruby books and a technical reviewer for several programming titles, he brings deep expertise and a keen eye for clarity, accuracy, and real-world applicability in technical publications.

Currently a Technical Fellow at LexisNexis, Eldon accelerates global software development practices by mentoring leaders, driving architectural improvements, and building tools in languages like Ruby and Go. His career includes leading technical transformations for enterprises across industries, fostering high-performing teams, and delivering scalable, maintainable software solutions.

Eldon's commitment to quality code and impactful mentorship makes him a trusted voice in the tech community, ensuring that developers of all levels can rely on his insights for learning and growth.

Acknowledgments

I owe a lot to Apress for taking up a topic that is not usually written about. Apress and Springer have long encouraged voices from the field, for which budding authors like us can only be grateful. I owe my thanks to Dr. Rozy Kamal, a very dear friend and scientist working in India, who understands how human beings work in organizations and whose 15+ years of work experience has been invaluable during the making of this book.

Suresh Konduru, who with his nearly 25 years of experience in the IT industry – extensively in Agile transformation, Agile consulting, Agile coaching and Scrum training, delivery management, program management, and project management for Global Fortune 500 customers – provided valuable insights into how Scrum alliance has been continuously shaping the world for the better.

I'd like to thank my reviewer, Eldon Alameda, who took the time to review my book. Connecting with code is one thing, connecting with someone else's philosophy and reviewing it is another.

Sanjay Sheoran has been a great senior with whom I discuss matters of organizational behavior. Devesh Khatri, a colleague and a friend, with whom case studies of people behavior and leadership came to life. Abhrajit Sarkar, who was one of the first senior leads where I learnt the value of meticulous detail. Murali, Sushma and Subba Rao, who continue to inspire my own agility. My teams – Bharat, Sagar, Vinay, Gagan, Mohit, Anima, Basit, Hiten, and Chander – we've learnt so much from each other. To my teachers in school – every book I write is because of the confidence you instilled in me in Loreto, Shimla. There have been countless others who through their experiences in the verticals of teaching, automobiles, nuclear science, software, finance, healthcare, and so many more have enriched me to write this book. If I have missed you in these acknowledgments, know that I am a student and a lifelong learner and you've been great teachers.

And none of this could have happened without my parents' example in agility. Our seniors are agile in many ways. Without sounding technical about it, there's so much to learn from them, including continuous improvement. Thank you so very much.

Introduction

Why I Wrote This Book

I simply seek to tap into our intuitive agility before we force fit ourselves into a framework, a manifesto, or a way of working. Most importantly, I wanted to address difficulties that teams were facing while adopting agile, Scrum in particular. I look into why agile is a social change before anything else. And in business, I look into what failed in principle that brought us to the Agile Manifesto, what values we need to uphold and seek within before tweaking industry standard frameworks, and what methods of working can help understand ourselves better. I wanted to understand how professionals are continuing in a broken world and why so. Packing all this into one book was a bold attempt, but I believe my readers will resonate with me, because your experiences and mine come from a broken world and human behavior.

Many companies are already tweaking Scrum, and for many, Agile exists in different flavors. This is not true for all companies of course. We have practitioners who follow the Scrum guide to the last word. However, I realized that some industry professionals simply do not resonate with Agile at all. They would give me flat answers – "It did not work for us." "We tried; it does not fit the bill." "We are comfortable without it, why should we switch at all?" And then came my personal experiences, where small companies thought they were being agile but were defeating agile completely. I wanted to understand where things were going wrong.

This book therefore became essential to voice my opinion to specify that if you are to modify existing frameworks in agile or create custom frameworks of your own (which I saw people doing), then at least don't defeat agile in principle. If you are adopting agile, from a non-agile background, don't think of it as a shift. It's within you already. A lot of thought has gone into the principles that the agile manifesto brings forth, and an equal amount of thought has gone into making its frameworks. Deep dive into what goes into a framework, and then, if you wish to customize a tried and tested way of doing things, go ahead with it.

Along the way, I also talk of where you'll fall when you defeat your own values for the sake of work. Who you are and what you become through work is a huge part of agility. We need to be agile in our regular lives. The words "human centric," "agile," "empiricism," and "Lean" have been used so often at work that people forget it's a part of them that is being appealed to through these philosophies and not an external organization or process. Since people have already reached the awareness that agile is a mindset, and not a process, we are not far from the day where we organize stress management through agile methods as well. Who knows! We've got to be agile in society; we've got to understand the word and implications on a cellular level and wherever that takes us.

Throughout my book, I have cited researchers' notes and voices from the field – not because I wanted to borrow from their understanding but because I wanted to highlight how different people have said the same thing through the ages. My citations, however, are not to be taken as an absolute. It is up to the reader to explore further and gain an understanding that resonates with the individual self. As is every other journey at work, your agile journey cannot be decoupled from your awareness of your higher self.

Who This Book Is For

This book is for leaders who appreciate governance models. Whether you're heading a cabinet in the government, a school, your home – the essentials remain the same. The commonalities in world progress would tell you that agile governance and human-centric approaches have led us to anything that we're proud of and how the lack of these two basic pointers have led to destruction of societies at large. In the book, we touch agility at a cellular level and at the level of national leadership. We speak of tapping the agility within and bringing it to your work. Most importantly, we speak of pushing the boundaries of agility, by respecting its true north. Custom agile frameworks should be treated as a way of looking at where the problem lies within organizations and processes and how to tap your best self for better outcomes. Hence, this book is for everyone who wishes to work with self-awareness.

What This Book Isn't

This book is not a manual for practitioners. It comes out of experience, and in the capacity of an agile coach – but not a guide to solve your particular business need. The author expresses her own opinion and hopes to solve problems that people might have faced in their careers.

CHAPTER 1

Introduction to Agile Alchemy and Customizing Agile

Haven't we heard of the buzzword agile for quite a while now? Industry veterans explaining it, practitioners adopting it, and students learning it. What can I say about it that has not been said yet? What can I write that has not been written before? Welcome to the playground. Welcome to the world of Agile Alchemy.

Businesses, teams, and individuals today are constantly faced with new challenges, shifting priorities, unexpected disruptions and demands of tough competition, and dynamic business cycles. It is not about following or breaking rules at all. It is about keeping an agile mindset. Being flexible, adaptive, continuously improving with honesty to self and motivation toward goals. It's about embodying being responsive to the unique needs of your context. Take this first chapter as more of a stage setting activity or just a conversation. Throughout the book, remember, that if you are agile (able to move quickly and easily, with progress), you can inspire agility. Let's begin!

© Kanika Sud 2025
K. Sud, *Customizable Agile Development*, https://doi.org/10.1007/979-8-8688-1055-8_1

Agility in Daily Life

Say it to yourself every time you implement a project with Agile methods – Agile is a mindset, a behavioral change; it's not a framework. Not a set way of working but remaining flexible with industry standard proven approaches in mind. Frameworks that are referred to as agile again and again are methods based on the underlying philosophy. Keep that difference, even when you talk to your teams.

We'll start with a short anecdote – yes. No projects for now. No industry. No job.

A small group of friends wanted to plan a trip to the mountains in Manali, India. They planned out the entire journey through the forest ahead of time. There was one young man who took charge, and the others looked up to him to plan the rest. "You'd map out a fixed route, gather all the supplies you think you'll need, and set off with the expectation of following your plan precisely, won't you?" – This was the question the group asked him. He made a plan and did what he understood best. And they started off. When they were following their plan, they met with unexpected obstacles in the forests of Manali. Wildlife they had not expected. Weather variations they had not prepared for. It was not what they had laid down in the plan.

The young man whom we mentioned in the beginning suddenly decided to continuously adapt and break the plan if necessary. His adaptation came from common sense, more than anything else. For instance, he told his friends, "Let's just not follow the plan as if it were the word of the Gospel. Let's start with a basic map and a compass...If you notice a shortcut or a beautiful clearing off the beaten path, you're open to exploring it, even if it wasn't in our initial plan. Just keep in mind to get the best out of this trip. If there is a weather variation, I am open to reprioritizing some of our tasks that we intended to do. Let's stick together for fear of wildlife around here. If possible, do you think we should ask one of the locals to guide us continuously?..."

This. This is agility at its simplest. In daily life.

In this agile approach, **you embrace uncertainty and change** as part of the journey. You **listen to input** from your fellow travelers, **learn from your experiences**, and **adjust** your direction accordingly. It's not about sticking to a fixed plan; it's about reaching your destination by being flexible, responsive, and adaptable. It's your approach that matters, not the destination alone.

Of course, our little story here might not appeal to students who wanted an example straight from the industry or a project-driven example. But then, that was the purpose of the section – to draw the attention of the reader toward an approach that is nimble, in life, not just at work. Lesson: *Through the lens of life, see how you work, and vice versa. Corporate culture cannot be defined as if we exist in companies only. Who we are as human beings takes up a lot of our behavior at office. It's that simple.*

Without knowing, human beings have always been agile. Here are some examples:

- You're preparing a special dinner for guests, following a complex recipe. However, you realize you're missing a key ingredient. You adapt your meal creatively using what you have in your kitchen. What you're doing here is agile. You've adapted.

- You've started learning a new language, and you encounter a difficult concept or technique. You decide you don't want to go by the book and answer quizzes, rather than experiment in learning the concept through ways that suit you best, maybe by increasing your reading and listening to relevant audio. What have you done here? You've chosen to be agile – choosing what best suits your final goal.

3

- While renovating a room in your home, you uncover an unexpected issue, like a hidden water leak. An agile solution to address the hidden water leak during my home renovation involves adapting the renovation process by incorporating the unexpected issue seamlessly. You'd immediately halt the renovation to prioritize assessing the extent and cause of the leak. With a flexible budget allocation, you'd allocate funds from the renovation budget to address the repair needs efficiently, without derailing the entire project. This may involve engaging professional plumbers or contractors, ensuring a proper and long-lasting fix. This agile approach would also allow for a flexible timeline, accommodating the time needed for the repairs and keeping the project on track while maintaining the overall quality of the renovation.

Cultivating an Agile Mindset

An agile mindset is not just about adaptability. We will revsisit the bible for agile enthusisasts again and again in the journey of this book - The Agile Manifesto. Let's go over the four values of the Agile Manifesto briefly and then adapt the same in daily life.

"Individuals and interactions over processes and tools."

So, in effect, if you make a conscious effort to value people, listen to them, understand how they can perform better and whether they are comfortable with processes, and let tools and processes be flexible enough for people to value, you are being agile. You're heading a unit, be it your family, your class in school, your team, or anything you think of – you cannot devalue people. Their challenges are yours to solve – and not through workarounds, through involvement. A good place to start is to see how you cater to your family's needs and assess yourself sharply at that, because families are what we easily take for granted.

"Working software over comprehensive documentation."

Working software has been mentioned because of the context of the manifesto's origin. But if you map this to a room you're decorating, what agility would you show? The working software is the actual interior here, as a deliverable, and its decoration is the requirement.

Let's list out a few points and see if we are being agile enough while still being able to follow the value quoted above.

- Prioritize the experience of being in the room, and adjust the decor based on real-time observations. If the room belongs to another person, understand and empathize with how he would like to live, rather than your thought of a home. The end user matters. It has to work for the person living in the room, visiting the room and visualizing the room. Remember, the comprehensive plan you made might not apply in later stages of the decoration project.

- Recalibrate and adjust as you go, changing things to improve the ambience, comfort, space utilization, and whatever works toward the final goal. This should make your approach outcome oriented. This shows willingness to change the plan as you go.

- Learn from experience, mistakes, as well as success. Find out what matters and what doesn't, what dissuades you from your goal, and what leads you to it. More on continuous improvement, in the next section.

"Customer collaboration over contract negotiation."

Let us, for a moment, stay away from any activity that involves business. Bring collaboration in your daily activities, not thinking of it as a job but a better way to get results. Imagine you are creating a garden for your home. You want all sorts of flowers – tiger lily, petunia, sunflower, marigold, and many more on that dream list of yours. Suddenly, you decide to let everyone collaborate in the activity by letting it be *inclusive*. What is this if not an agile mindset? If you share information about these flowers and gather knowledge about more kinds of plants from other members of the family and the gardeners – you would then be *collaborative*. In this example, the collaborators are not exactly customers, but they are involved in the holistic experience of making the garden a success. What about contract negotiation? Well, if somewhere in the middle of everything your work involves adding another spot to the initial agreement and your scope of work increases, it should not let work come to a halt. A person who makes the initial agreement as the problem, rather than incorporating a solution around the latest development, is creating a challenge and is a barrier to agility.

"Responding to change over following a plan."

Embrace changes as opportunities. If a piece of furniture doesn't fit as expected, you need to keep in mind that the home you make should work for you or whomever is going to live in it – not just adhering to a predefined exhaustive plan. In fact, a deeper look at "responding to change" would help you understand your growth, rather than react to change. When you are responding to change, the sharper your observation, the better the chances of a good response. If the response occurs without observing the self and others, it is more of a reaction headed in the wrong direction.

These values are not just about agility in management, they make you a better person if you truly apply them to your place of work and to regular life. It's ultimately the mind you're talking of, and that means that Agile is what the mind makes of it.

Learning and Continuous Improvement in Life Outside Work

People who are successful are the ones who learn continuously, *without arrogance*. We had to emphasize without arrogance, because learning and knowledge does take you on the path of a know-it-all. You won't be able to step back until you do a self-check continuously. Just two days before I wrote this section, I was reading *How Life Imitates Chess* by Garry Kasparov. Kasparov's book draws fascinating parallels between the strategies and tactics used in chess and the challenges we face in everyday life. The objective, however, is not to digress and take you to the game of chess. The idea is to help you choose imbibe values from life to work and back. Here are a few excerpts:

> *Experience and knowledge are focused through the prism of talent, which itself can be pushed, pulled and cultivated. This mix is the source of intuition, an absolutely unique tool for each of us. Here we begin to see the influence of individual psychology and our emotional make-up expressed in our decisions – what we call style in a chess player.*

> *I wanted to blaze new trails, even if at that point in my life that meant little more than taking a new route on the walk home. And throughout my chess career I sought out new challenges, looking for things no one had done before.*

> *We must look higher and dig deeper, move beyond the basic and universal.*

> *Acquired patterns and the logic to employ them, combine with our inherent qualities to create a unique decision-maker.*

> *Self-awareness is essential to being able to combine your knowledge, experience and talent to reach your peak performance.*

> —From *How Life Imitates Chess* by Garry Kasparov

Now, stop and think, if life can imitate chess, can't life imitate the line of work you choose to represent? And that too in the strongest possible, positive ways? In fact, if for some reason, your life, learning, and interest are far apart from the work you do, you know there is a problem. Learning happens faster when you do something of your interest, and that is why love for your work is a precursor to self-improvement. True happiness for dedicated professionals is a function of effective process and interesting work, not just the result itself. There are millions and billions of people in wrong jobs, toxic cultures – think of it, identifying how you learn best and what is of your interest will only take you to the right goal. The lack of mind wellness is closely related to the lack of growth which ultimately leads to the lack of agility. Target holistic wellness if you are ever to resonate with principles of true leadership – any industry can suck you faster than you think.

Garry Kasparov spoke of philosophy from his chosen profession. So can you. The man speaks from a level of consciousness. He never stopped learning and understanding his own game and his opponent's as well. If you read this book, you'll come across an interesting anecdote where he narrates how after 5 months, 48 games, and thousands of hours of play and study, the match was declared over forcefully, without a winner. He came back, however, and used all his learning in all those games and applied it. Observation was what he practiced and it got him where he was.

Let us also mention learning through journaling. Personal retrospectives for understanding your own progress are a highly underrated tool. Later in this book, we present dedicated templates about how to understand your growth and development, personally and professionally. For now, know that if you are to continually learn and grow, it's a good idea to start penning down "what" you've learnt from an experience, "why" you feel the need to keep the lesson, and "how" you can implement it further. Again, pen it down...don't keep it in your memory box. Some think that consciously recognizing a concept helps it stay in memory. For how long, you may ask? We won't get into deep specifics, but habituation and associative learning are two techniques that human cells learn by, among others. These terms are self-descriptive. Habituation means getting acquainted to one or more stimuli, and associative learning is about how cells link two or more stimuli. There are other mechanisms to describe this, but the key goal is to identify how you learn. Once you spot ways of learning and grasping, you'll no longer be stuck. The leader in you will be far more effective. You will inspire learning as well. Most importantly, you would know what to improve in yourself. What we are speaking of here will be revisited in the last chapter again, where the neuroscience of agile is explored as a separate topic. Let us just close this section by saying that continuous improvement cannot exist without self-observation.

Where Agility Sets in for Businesses

From daily life, we now come to workplaces. The fundamental of everything we propose in this book is that work cannot be isolated from life. It's not as if the moment you set foot in office, you become agile, and when you clock out, you let the principles of agile die. Effective leaders empower their teams by fostering an environment where creativity and risk-taking are encouraged. They provide the necessary resources, guidance, and psychological safety for team members to explore new ideas, iterate on processes, and learn from failures. By setting the right tone and leading by example, leaders inspire agility and adaptability. It's almost as if everyone is committed to follow what makes sense toward a common goal. That is exactly why going through the Agile Manifesto is important. It sets the tone right.

In a company where I worked, there was a leadership seminar, where a team member was asked to make a tower out of building blocks, but he was blindfolded. There was an observer, who noted observations on how the team member executed the task under instructions from the team manager, and a team lead. The objective of stating this here is that you are bound to get so absorbed in daily life and work that observing yourself might not be the most obvious response from your mind. If, however, you observe your actions and seek self-awareness and collaboration, you're bound to build a strong tower. Not surprisingly, there was one out of six teams that built the tower according to the committed height, and this team worked according to some very minute details:

- The blindfolded executive used the smallest unit measurement (the crease lines on a finger) to understand where the blocks were placed, from where he was seated. There was a strategy in place but not a granular plan that could not be altered later.

- The executive learnt from guidance as well when one of his blocks fell down.

- The team manager's guidance was minimal and objective but extremely helpful.

- The team manager knew when to step back and when to guide.

- The team lead's communication was animated, and unnecessary in places, but was collaborative indeed.

- The team committed a length of 12 blocks and reached 14 and stopped by mutual consensus.

- Just like cells communicate with each other by sending and receiving signals, which can come from the environment or other cells – the freshly formed team started communicating along pathways that were immediately available to them. For instance, the team lead was available for the executive. The manager was available for the lead. As we will see in Chapter 5, communication and its methods help a lot in shaping teams and groups.

I was an observer for this team, and as I saw in the months ahead, the people of this group were some of the most consistent colleagues I've worked with. What I concluded from the activity was the following:

- It is easier to observe others than observe yourself. You are so engrossed in daily work that you are literally blindfolded, aren't you. Walk out of yourself, take out time for retros, and think how you could do better.

- Keeping metrics for successful progress and keeping them simple and small will help you understand whether you are doing it right at the basics.

- A major sign of good communication is that it is well received, well understood, and helpful.

- When to lead and when to step back is a measure of management and leadership.

- The plan and the goal might change, but your progress should not be affected by it.

- Adhere to the timelines and deliverables you committed. Don't overcommit. Commitment according to what you can do and living up to it is a sign of integrity.

- Teams that produce results often do so, without friction.

What Is Agile Alchemy, Then?

The reader might wonder that if agile itself is about remaining flexible, why introduce a fantastical concept of "magic" or "alchemy" in it? Alchemy roughly translates to magic or an ancient way that dealt with trying to find a way to change ordinary metals into gold. So, what is that word doing here? The sadness of the industry or rather the humans who adopt a mindset get stuck inside that mindset, which in a way is justified, because it has taken researchers' time and thought to arrive at a conclusion regarding such research. It cannot be trifled with, and what is adopted, the Scrum framework for instance, is adopted without underlying principles. Here sets in the sadness. People forget that agile itself encourages the world to keep reinnovating. So, keep trying to make a framework into an intentionally evolving framework, which can be a truly agile method. That, dear reader, is where the alchemy sets in.

Breaking Agile for Being Agile? No!

"Breaking Agile" doesn't mean abandoning Agile principles. It's about recognizing that Agile is not a one-size-fits-all solution and that it should be tailored to specific contexts. This concept encourages teams to be pragmatic and to prioritize what works best for their particular situation while still upholding the core values of Agile, such as collaboration, customer-centricity, and continuous improvement.

In essence, "Breaking Agile for Being Agile" underscores the essence of agility itself—being able to pivot, adapt, and evolve as circumstances demand while staying true to the principles that promote effective and efficient project delivery. It's a reminder that Agile is a means to an end, not an end in itself.

Summary

So now, we have a fair idea of what agile is. We also have a fair hint of why we need to keep evolving keeping in mind the Agile Manifesto. The idea is to break away from rigid adherence to rituals when it becomes counterproductive for Agile principles. It emphasizes the importance of flexibility, adaptability, and a focus on outcomes over processes.

In the next chapter, we introduce how Agile is being practiced as of now and how these methods came about – how people were frustrated without them and why it's important to observe the cocreators of agile methods thought process. Let's dive into the next chapter, because what lies ahead is quite a recipe in the making.

Further Reading

On Agility
On Culture
How Life Imitates Chess

Exercise

Create a journal, and write down three things at the end of every week – mapping the following:

- What I did well

- What I could have done better

- What inspired me

CHAPTER 2

Agile Forerunners and the Stories of Scrum and Kanban

In the previous chapter, we introduced agility and very slightly and gave a hint of what is meant by being agile rather than following agile. It was easy to point out that agility is a mindset. The goal of this chapter is to establish a strong foundation about agile frameworks. We start from the evolution of Agile and walk up to primary Agile methods in use today. While the "Further Reading" section promises a lot of useful links, we recommend that you supplement the reading of this chapter with as much material as possible, from online sources and courses.

Start with Why: Evolution of Agile

In Chapter 1, the section "Cultivating an Agile Mindset" spoke about the daily application of the agile value system. Here, we touch on points which bring about why agile is needed as a philosophy at work. If you have no information on the evolution of agile, specifically about linear, spiral, hybrid, and unified models of management, we'd recommend you'd study more about these models on the web. A simple wiki information would put you into the right context. For now, just remember that these models

© Kanika Sud 2025
K. Sud, *Customizable Agile Development*, https://doi.org/10.1007/979-8-8688-1055-8_2

tested values of the people implementing these frameworks, and that is where they failed. Also, every model's failure became the "why" of its successor.

Thus, agility evolved as a need, after a few mandatory values were consciously identified by a group of people managing solution delivery.

Before you read our high-level summary of evolving methods, Figures 2-1 and 2-2 provide a glance at the visual representations of two very early models that literally put developers into trouble.

Waterfall Method

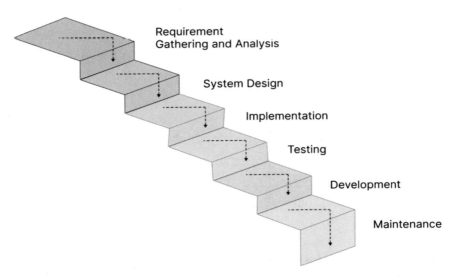

Figure 2-1. *Waterfall Model – Linear Strategy, No Jumping Back*

V Model

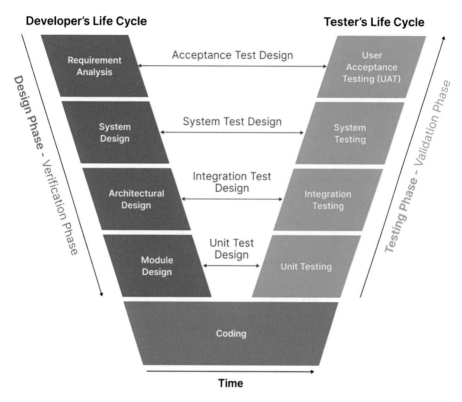

Figure 2-2. *The V-Model of Management*

We'll now explain both the models in a moment. What happened in waterfall was that people spent a lot of time in planning upfront, and those plans never came to fruition. The main problems of the waterfall method turned out to be as follows:

- It defeated the very idea of transparency. Who does not want transparency? Which client would not want to look at what is being developed? The lack of demonstrated progress was a serious lag in this model, as the customer was not ready to see visible progress.

17

Stakeholders were typically only involved during the initial requirements phase and at the end, leaving little opportunity for feedback during development. Again, bookmark the word transparency. We shall later describe the case study of the VCF in FBI, which will shed more light on this.

- Testing came very late into the process, and teams were running into hellholes of verifying issues. Whether you follow waterfall or not, if issues are not identified on time and your metrics are not in place, your problems might scale right under your nose, without you noticing it. The problem is never the bug; the problem is the unwillingness of teams to discover bugs early in the process. Now, for a bigger case study, take the example of NASA's Mars Climate Orbiter (1999). On September 23, 1999, communication with the spacecraft was permanently lost during its orbital insertion. As it approached Mars, it followed a trajectory that brought it too close to the planet, resulting in its destruction in the atmosphere or its escape into an orbit around the Sun. The project failed due to a unit mismatch between two teams (metric vs. imperial). Here again, Edward Weiler, NASA associate administrator for space science said clearly, "The problem here was not the error; it was the failure of NASA's systems engineering, and the checks and balances in our processes, to detect the error. That's why we lost the spacecraft."

- It was simply inflexible to change. Every change was first taken up as a contract negotiation and then anything else. Now, as a framework, nobody can compel you to take up scope creep without contract negotiation. The people who implement such models create the rigidity around it. Note that when you are fixed to a box and you can't go back on what you've done – or going back involves cost – the stakes rise, and blame games begin. That's what happened in most implementations. I've been part of projects where if a requirement changed, and once it did (in a web app that required 10,000 URLs to be automated for content change), the process was inflexible to not allow that change. Everyone was at a loss, because nobody expected change at all.

- No milestones within the entire cycle meant that there was a high risk of obsolescence or failure. The UK National Health Service (NHS) IT Modernization (2002–2011) aimed to digitize patient records but was ultimately abandoned after spending over £10 billion. The long development cycle and late visibility into progress led to a solution that did not meet users' needs.

Leave alone product development, you'd not want a life so rigid that it does not leave room for change.

Then people shifted to the V-Model, but that lacked the value of transparency too. This is how. The V-Model is a software development life cycle (SDLC) model that resembles a V shape. Like waterfall, it follows a strict, sequential approach where each phase of development is completed before moving onto the next. On the left side of the "V" are the development phases. The right side of the V mirrors these phases with corresponding testing activities. The V-Model did not involve the client early in the cycle of development and lacked continuous feedback from the client – which meant no voice for stakeholder opinion. This model did however involve iterative testing, which was beneficial for the project and is used till date.

Right up to here, models did not profess demos. **There was also a huge emphasis on documentation, over and above the deliverable. This entire problem led to the exhaustion of teams, who finally became the flag-bearers of lightweight but robust methods in development.** The kind of documentation made upfront, like Gantt charts, for instance, assumed that developers would be able to live up to the plan. Plans change, and when they do, you'd have to rework through the plan.

Then came the sawtooth model (Figure 2-3), which includes client interaction at meaningful times.

Saw Tooth Model

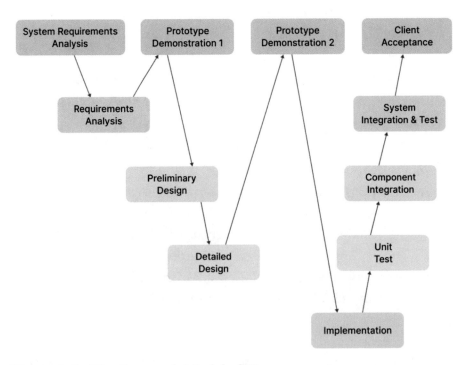

Figure 2-3. *The Sawtooth Model of Management*

What makes the sawtooth model distinct is that it distinguishes between the client and the development team. In this model, tasks requiring the client's presence and tasks only requiring the development team are made distinct. The inherent problems however were more related to time. And time is money, as we all know. There was no guide which would say how long the activities should go on. Teams needed a torch, so to speak, someone to tell them how to come out of one phase and when to close it. I have been part of teams, which would go on and on with design and never come to code. There were other problems, such as scope creep. In all linear models, the emphasis was on getting the requirements right, upfront, and not changing them afterward. A compromise on any requirement would lead to more frustration in some or the other form.

Iterative models thus evolved and can be considered as forerunners to truly agile practices, and yet, they also embody sequential steps, reminiscent of previous linear processes.

The biggest advantage that iterative models brought to the table was that you could loop back to the previous step. This shift was recognized as a good shift. What was good was taken forward, and what was inconvenient was dropped.

Let's start now, with the spiral model, as shown in Figure 2-4.

Spiral Model

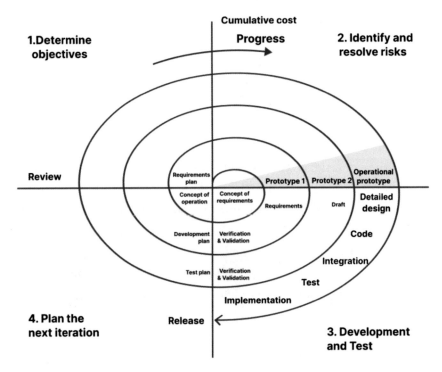

Figure 2-4. Spiral Model

Explaining the spiral model is out of the scope of this book, but we'd recommend that you look it up online (link given at the end of the chapter), and here, we'll give you a brief. The spiral model was introduced by Barry Boehm in 1986; it was outlined as a basic process for design and implementation, by revisiting phases of the process, after they've been completed. Think of four quadrants and each of these four quadrants, as a phase of an iteration. You can call it a journey where you continuously assess risks, build prototypes, evaluate progress, and adapt plans, with huge emphasis on risk assessment (and hence it's suitability for risk heavy projects). You move forward in cycles, not a straight line, embracing both the structure of phases and the flexibility of iteration. It's a powerful approach for complex projects, ensuring you reach the summit with a product that stands the test of time.

Risk assessment ultimately became a drawback for smaller projects where the process of analyzing risks was costly, and unless risk analysis was extremely necessary, the spiral model became less frequently used. Also, in the spiral model, you could not reprioritize the amount of work left to be done. Completing tasks and deliverables within each phase is crucial before moving on, creating a more structured progression, which prevents complete flexibility. Moreover, customer centricity was still not in the picture, because demos and reviews were not explicitly stated, like you can see in the picture above.

And now, the last model that we discuss in this chapter – the unified process model (UPM). The unified process model lays emphasis on architecture, iterations, and use cases. UPM prioritizes architecture and use cases in its software development approach. This means it focuses on creating a solid foundation for the software and ensuring it caters to specific user needs, both at the core of each iteration and the overall project. Both Agile and UPM share some overlap in their values, particularly regarding iterative development, user focus, and continuous improvement. However, teams still struggled with contract negotiations and robust delivery, over and above heavy weight documentation. Here's a breakdown of what it typically includes:

- **Inception Phase:** The starting point where requirements are gathered and feasibility is assessed

- **Elaboration Phase:** Further refinement of requirements, architecture, and project risks

- **Construction Phase:** The main development stage, with iterative cycles to build and refine the system

- **Transition Phase:** Final testing, deployment, and user training

- **Iterations:** Short cycles of development that occur throughout the phases, with emphasis on continuous testing and feedback

For a visual representation of UPM, check Figure 2-5 below.

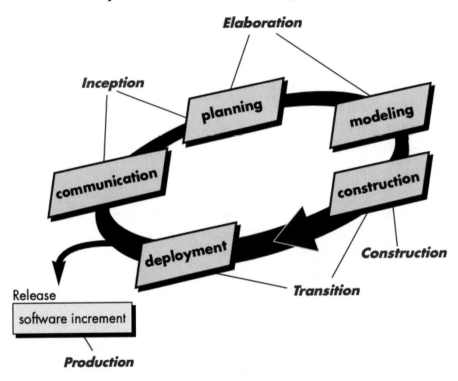

Figure 2-5. *The Unified Process Model*
Image source: Medium | The Unified Process by Juan Abaroa

A key thing to note about linear models is that the scope is largely fixed and the timeline to deliver a chunk of the work was flexible. Agile inverted this philosophy on top of its head. It said, let's keep the scope flexible (within bounds of acceptance), and let's keep the time for delivering a chunk of the work fixed.

There might be many ways you describe a philosophy, but it's notable to see how Atlassian Corporation, a leader in its development of products for management, puts the importance of adopting a philosophy rather than the choice of framework.

> *[...]However, after more than a decade of helping agile teams get work done at Atlassian, we've learned that clear communication, transparency, and a dedication to continuous improvement should always remain at the center of whatever framework you choose. And the rest is up to you.*

> —Atlassian Blogs on Agile

Another thing that could really help readers is to understand stories of Agile Manifesto Signatories. These stories tell us where they came from and why the history of software development cannot be undermined. It prepares you for the future – rightly put by Jim Highsmith, a coauthor of the Agile Manifesto, a founding member of Agile Alliance, coauthor of the Declaration of Interdependence for project leaders, and cofounder and first president of the Agile Leadership Network. In this video hyperlinked here, Jim presents his opinion on why lightweight methods of software development were needed. Jim talks about the history of the Agile Manifesto and how technology has changed software development. He also discusses the seven wastes of software development and how to eliminate them. We will talk of them in the next chapter on Lean.

Come to think of it, technology became lightweight, and software supporting it too. And it was only natural that the Agile Manifesto, which was signed by 17 software development practitioners at a conference in Snowbird, Utah, in February 2001 was seen as a step toward moving off heavy weight that adds to waste. These individuals, who were known as "lightweight methodologists," came together to discuss ways to improve software development practices. By lightweight, the reader should not assume small projects, as will become evident through the case studies we present, but only a step away from rigidity. Through 2 days of deliberation, they formulated a set of 4 values and 12 principles that they believed could enhance the effectiveness of software development teams. Motivated by a shared desire to improve the industry, these individuals signed the Agile Manifesto, which has since become a cornerstone of modern software development methodologies.

The conference was held at Snowbird Resort, a ski resort in Utah. The attendees were able to spend time skiing and snowboarding together, which helped to build camaraderie and trust. As a matter of coincidence, they were dealing with similar problems. This was proof enough that if problems were similar, a solution must be round the corner. Again, you need the passion to discuss work and have work first conversations, rather than treat organizational culture as mere gossip. It's people who are concerned about problems, who bring in solutions. "Culture eats strategy for breakfast" is a famous quote from legendary management consultant and writer Peter Drucker. This is so true, because even now, people try to follow agile with a waterfall mindset! They'd play blame games in the name of accountability. They would want more documents than deliverables. Their insecurity around documents stems from the fact that tech excellence is not a concern for them at all, leave alone motivation. People want to understand agile, as a practice not as a culture. Yet, ironically, speak to any one of the signatories of the manifesto and you'll know how agile is first a culture, followed by an umbrella of activities.

A last reminder before we delve into agile frameworks: Map the principles and values in the Agile Manifesto to each framework as we go along.

Scrum and Kanban: Unveiling the Agile Duo

We now start looking at the two major Agile frameworks that everybody has heard of, while evaluating their values and how their thought process works. It's the thought behind the framework that matters. Not just following the framework without it's philosophy.

Scrum

The one word that every agile practitioner has heard the most.
A purposefully incomplete framework that speaks of lightweight documentation, borrows from its predecessor frameworks, and moves forward through empiricism. Before we speak of the framework, however, let's narrate here a story of Jeff Sutherland's (the cocreator of Scrum along with Ken Schwaber) days as a fighter pilot. Here's an excerpt from Jeff's interview with Sean Ammirati for Agile Giants. Notice how Jeff speaks of completely different things – fighter jets and the mathematical model of human cells – and connects adaptation to both. Read on.

> *You know, Scrum derives from 11 years of fighter pilot training. I was a fighter pilot in the Air Force and in fact this weekend I was at the Air Force center for figuring out how to get the entire Air Force Agile. And it's all based on John Boyd, the world's greatest fighter pilot and what is called the OODA loop: **observe, orient, decide, act**, how to respond quickly and dynamically in the environment. That's the operational piece of Scrum. … I wound up as a professor of mathematics at the Air Force Academy and completed my doctoral work at the nearest medical school at the time. So that led to an 11-year career as a professor of radiology at the University of Colorado School of Medicine. And there I had millions of dollars every year from the national cancer institute to mathematically model the human cell. And learning about what causes a cell to change, we were particularly interested in what causes cancer, led me into the study of complex adaptive systems and evolutionary biology. And realizing that any system, whether it's a cell, a person, or a team is a complex adaptive system and will migrate through the state space of functionality. Either in a positive or a negative direction. Because of small changes that are caused by incidents that occur that effect the environment.*
>
> —Jeff Sutherland (read full interview on Agile Giants, Medium)

What is obvious is that fighter jets can't stick to any plan; they've got to adapt according to dynamic changes. Boyd had skillfully observed that two design choices in fighter jets led to a higher success rate for American planes over the Soviet planes. These two design choices effectively led American pilots see better and respond faster. Their cockpits had fewer blind spots due to their bubble design and their controls were fully hydraulic. To be able to see better and respond faster according to what you see makes the ground for *adaptation* **and** *transparency*. In another episode, on one of his own trips, Jeff required information while maneuvering blows, and he realized that what would work is a single snapshot at any given time, to get an idea about what he wanted to know with respect to the entire journey. Later, he introduced this very concept in Scrum reporting – the Burndown Chart, which acts as a visual tool to track the remaining work in a sprint or project over time. It helps teams monitor progress toward completion, ensuring alignment with sprint goals and promoting transparency.

The word Scrum borrows from the Rugby approach, and now we get to defining it.

Figure 2-6 defines Scrum, and even though this book does not intend to be a guide for Scrum, we shall detail it out for you and map it to the interview given by Sutherland, as cited above. See the image below.

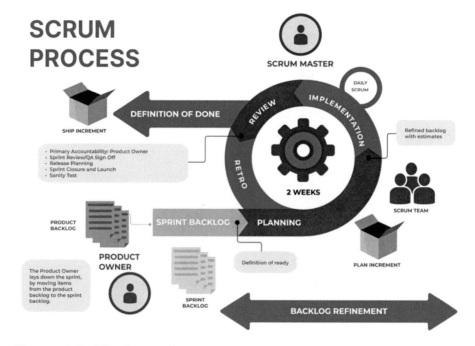

Figure 2-6. *The Scrum Process*

Image credits: https://www.instagram.com/animaagrawal.design/
The components which make up Scrum are given below.

Scrum Definition

Components

For clarity, let's define the workflow. Scrum has five events (Sprint, Sprint
Planning, Sprint Review, Sprint Retrospective, and Daily Standup),
three artifacts (Product Backlog, Sprint Backlog, and Increment), three
accountabilities (Scrum Master, Product Owner, and Scrum Team), and
five Scrum values (Commitment, Focus, Openness, Respect, and Courage).
Again, it is to be noted how values were not undermined just for the sake
of a framework. We will go further into the events, in the next section while
defining artifacts.

Scrum is founded on empiricism and lean thinking. Empiricism asserts that knowledge comes from experience and making decisions based on what is observed. Lean thinking reduces waste and focuses on the essentials.

—Scrum Guide Online

Artifacts

Let's start with artifacts and then events, and see where they are placed in the workflow, and while describing the workflow, we'll discuss the pillars of Scrum – Inspection, Adaptation, and Transparency.

The first step is to put down all requirements and break them down in unit structures. This tells you what lies ahead. It is called the **Product Backlog**. It is the single source of work undertaken by the Scrum Team, in an ordered list. For people coming from traditional project management or waterfall methods – you can think of this as a Work Breakdown Structure, only that, among other factors, it is more agile and can be changed as per the end user's needs without contractual negotiations.

> **Sprint Goal or the Increment**: The Sprint Goal is the shippable chunk of the product that the team commits to delivering at the end of a specific period (spanning one week or two weeks), namely the Sprint. It should be chosen such that every Increment moves you closer to the monthly or quarterly goal and is additive toward the previous Increment.

> **Sprint Backlog**: Out of your Product Backlog, comes a set of items that you can ship in a week or two. The set of items is called Sprint Backlog. The Sprint Backlog is tied to the Sprint Goal, in that it cannot be considered delivered **until the Sprint Goal meets the Definition of Done**. Recheck the figure above.

From the Product Backlog, the Product Owner pulls in stories to the Sprint Backlog. The team questions the stories and checks if they are in a state of "readiness" to begin execution. Such sessions are called backlog grooming sessions and can happen any time, ideally before the sprint execution begins. Once the "Definition of Ready" is passed, the stories are moved to Sprint Planning. Note that backlog grooming and definition of ready are not officially defined in the Scrum Guide, but smooth execution is not really possible without these two workflow checkpoints.

Let's say you already have the requirements by now. You have a fair idea of what the product is about. What would you do in a product life cycle? Now, to arrive at a cost, you'd take a fair idea of the timeline. Even though Scrum itself doesn't define a specific road map document, the industry practices a Sprint-based road map, to understand the timeline of the entire project, grouped by Sprint. Figure 2-7 shows a product road map, following sprints, making it clear which feature would be developed by when.

Feature	Epic	User Stories	Sprint 1	Sprint 2	Sprint 3	Sprint 4
Role Group Management						
		Add Role Group with Super Admin				
		Role Group Association With Contract/Global Scope				
		Add Role Group With SaaS Admin				
	Adding a Role Group	Role group Role Association According to Scope and Contract				
		Edit Role Group				
		Cloning Role Group				
	Editing a Role group	Hide/Unhide Role Groups				
		Search Role Groups wccording to Privelege				
	Search Role Groups	HIPPA Compliance Within Search				
User Management						
		Azure B2C User Creation				
	Add User	Add User				
		Edit User Profile				
		Edit User Role Information				
		Reset Registration				
		Unlock User				
	Edit User	Delete User				

Figure 2-7. *A Sample Product Road Map*

The product road map covers broadly which modules are going to be covered in which sprints and how are they panned out in the project life cycle.

Events

Sprint: The container event is a cycle of time, mutually agreed to by the Scrum Team and the Product Owner and Scrum Master, to deliver a shippable chunk of the whole product. All of execution happens in this one event. The scope can be clarified with the Product Owner, but the Sprint timeline should remain the same. This helps you understand how much you can deliver in each cycle of time, as a team. Estimation of tasks is a whole deep conversation altogether. For this, we recommend backlog refinement sessions, where you continue to refine the backlog, and as a team, you can reprioritize and redefine requirements with better acceptance criteria. This container event tests all your values – such as Commitment, Focus, Openness, Respect, and Courage. It's the real meat of the rugby match.

Sprint Planning: This is where you refine, define, prioritize, and estimate what you are going to do in the Sprint. This requires a lot of focus. The more focused you are, the better you manage. Go back to Figure 2-6, and you'll see that the checkpoint after every event denotes a difference in your progress. After Sprint Planning, the backlog is estimated and defined as "ready" for implementation. Note that Scrum does not guide on how to estimate. That power is given to a team, for autonomy. Many are in favor, and many teams often long for good estimation practices. When we create custom frameworks, we shall see how estimations can be refined.

Daily Standup: This forms part of how you go about the execution. Talk about your day's plan, impediments, progress, backlog, estimations, and progress for a typical 15–30 min, and wrap it up. Turning up every day to discuss progress, at the same time, and keeping it time boxed is one of the highest notes on Commitment toward your goal. The way such a meeting is conducted speaks of the team's values, including servant leadership and courage.

Sprint Review: This is where you look at what you've made and you present it to stakeholders. Openly sharing progress fosters trust and alignment, and this encourages transparency. The Sprint Review isn't just a showcase; it's a critical feedback loop. It should not be avoided at any rate. For the road map listed in Figure 2-7, Sprint 1 review would happen in front of the stakeholders at the end of Week 3. Mid Sprint-check ins are also popular. The idea is to fail fast, so that bugs and problems and questions are discovered earlier in the cycle.

Sprint Retro: The one event that tests your honesty to yourself. Identify where you could have done better. This tests the value of empiricism, as it inspires learning from experience.

If you've noticed, if you have the right balance of Commitment, Focus, Openness, Respect, and Courage, Scrum gives you a good canvas for plugging in Inspection, Transparency, and Adaptation (Empiricism, remember?) at every stage. A special mention to the retrospective ceremony here, in that the retrospective ceremony can be played out in so many ways that you can really be a better person at the end of it. All it takes is honesty with yourself. We will come to exploring techniques of retrospectives when we innovate agile practices. Also, see how the Sprint Retrospective and the Sprint Review support the idea of the OODA loop.

Let's now move to the accountabilities.

Actors/Accountabilities

In a team where team ownership is hailed, the real world with a job at stake cries for accountability matrices. And that is why you need to know who is doing what.

Product Owner: The single entity who owns the vision, owns the backlog, and owns transparency.

The Product Owner is responsible for the following:

- Defining and clearly communicating the Product Goal, which sets the overall direction for the product.

- Creating and elaborating Product Backlog items, ensuring they are clear, concise, and valuable. It is to be noted that defining Product Backlog items are only under the accountability of the Product Owner; it is still the responsibility of the whole Scrum Team. Though the Scrum Guide does not speak of acceptance criteria, giving acceptance criteria is the accountability of the Product Owner, but the whole Scrum Team can take part in such activities, which would further enhance collaboration and understanding.

- Ordering the Product Backlog items based on priority and business value.

- Maintaining transparency and visibility of the Product Backlog, making it readily accessible to all stakeholders.

Scrum Master: The primary facilitator of Scrum. He will coach teams, remove their impediments, understand the nature of business stories, and understand technicalities and everything under the umbrella of Sprint implementation. The Scrum Master gathers players and props for each act – planning, dailies, reviews, and reflections. A Scrum Master's role is vast. The Scrum Master wears many hats, serving different parties within the Agile ecosystem. For the Scrum Team, he is a coach, nurturing self-management and cross-functionality while ensuring high-value deliveries adhering to the "Definition of Done." They're also a tireless advocate, clearing roadblocks and fostering productive, time-boxed Scrum events. For the Product Owner, the Scrum Master becomes a partner, aiding in understanding the use cases and getting things done. They help the team embrace concise backlog items and develop empirical planning strategies for even the most complex environments. On a larger scale, the Scrum Master can become an agile coach for adopting agile principles to ensure that teams are indeed agile. He is a multifaceted force driving successful Scrum adoption for high-performing teams.

Scrum Team

This is possibly the most difficult team to structure and is an ongoing debate when it comes to deciding between a generalist agile team, v/s a specialist agile team. The one thing that Scrum does recommend is that strong Scrum Teams are self-organizing and approach their projects with a clear "we" attitude and are cross-functional. Everyone in the team should be aware of task reviews, continuous delivery, and release cadences. Shared skill sets have been observed to be the key foundation of cross-functional teams, and the best way to understand specialization agnostic functioning is to be aware of the value that a particular activity returns in the PM cycle.

The accountability matrix can also be laid down as shown in Figure 2-8.

	Product Owner	SM	Scrum Team
Backlog Refinement	Co-Owns	Co-Owns	Co-Owns
Agile Estimation	Participates	Facilitates	Owns
Sprint Planning	Co-Owns	Facilitates	Co-Owns
Daily Scrum	Participates	Facilitates	Participates
Sprint Review	Owns	Participates	Participates (Need not be present if the SM can demo)
Sprint Retro	Helps	Facilitates	Owns

Figure 2-8. *Accountability Matrix in Scrum*

It is to be noted that the makers of Scrum say that the responsibility is equal, but the accountability is divided between roles.

Go back to the interview that was presented earlier in this chapter, where Jeff spoke of teams, cells, and organizations being complex adaptive systems, which are affected by change. Jeff understood that change is inevitable and constantly growing through change will need to be a philosophy of the framework and the mindset of the people who follow it.

I revisit the Scrum Guide every month, and trust me, I see some things that I never did before, in a new light. Take this line, for instance, which is my latest favorite:

> *Various practices exist to forecast progress, like burn-downs, burn-ups, or cumulative flows. While proven useful, these do not replace the importance of empiricism. In complex environments, what will happen is unknown. Only what has already happened may be used for forward-looking decision making.*

> —Scrum Guide, 2020

World Famous Case Studies in Lack of Agility

Healthcare.gov

Let's explore the case study of Healthcare.gov, a federal resource specifically designed to guide residents in states for the United States without their own health insurance marketplaces to compare and purchase private plans. It is a prime example of a project that suffered from a lack of agility and paid the price. Launched in October 2013, Healthcare.gov was tasked with facilitating signups for millions of Americans seeking health insurance under the ACA. The project was massive, complex, and involved multiple government agencies and contractors. Like we said, agility is not just for smaller projects, and lightweight should not be mistaken for the size of the project. Even the biggest of blunders could have been solved with agile principles, and the biggest of successes are based on the same agile and lean thinking. (We'll introduce lean soon.) The Office of Inspector General clearly stated in its report that a high degree of uncertainty about mission, scope, and funding affected the project from the start. On launch day, the website was riddled with glitches and errors, rendering it unusable for many users. Months passed before critical issues were resolved, leading to public outcry and political pressure. Here, we start by giving key takeaways from the report that affected the downfall of the project, and then, we attempt to relate it with our daily lives. HHS (Department of Health and Human Services) had overall responsibility for the project, including policy setting, budget allocation, and stakeholder engagement. However, the actual development and management of the website fell under CMS (Centers for Medicare & Medicaid Services). CMS held the direct contract and management responsibility for building and launching the website. This included responsibilities like selecting contractors, managing development, and conducting testing. All of the points have been quoted directly from the report found here: `https://oig.hhs.gov/oei/reports/oei-06-14-00350.pdf`.

- On October 1, 2013, HealthCare.gov experienced 250,000 concurrent users, much greater than the planned capacity. Website outages began within two hours of launch, preventing many consumers from logging in and signing up for health insurance. In the end, only six consumers were able to submit an application and select a plan on the first day of the first open enrollment. **Defects, therefore, were not treated as wastage or a sign of rework – leading to bad quality.**

- Most critical was the absence of clear leadership, which caused delays in decision-making, and lack of clarity in project tasks. CMS leaders and staff failed to recognize the magnitude of problems, became **resistant to bad news about the website's development**, and **failed to act on warnings and address problems**.

- Missteps included **devoting too much time to developing policy**, which left too little time for developing the website.

- CMS's organizational structure and culture also hampered progress, including poor coordination between policy and technical work and **reluctance to alter plans in the face of problems**. Straightforward lack of agility.

- CMS continued a failing path to developing HealthCare.gov despite signs of trouble.

- As problems worsened, CMS staff and contractors became path dependent, continuing to follow the same plan and schedule rather than change course as circumstances warranted.

- A CMS technical advisor and two consulting firms identified specific problems that threatened a successful launch. Attempts by CMS to take action on recommendations were poorly executed.

These were some of the main causes of the apparent failure to launch the website correctly in 2013.

If you look closely at the lessons learned section in the report, given in the figure below, **you'll see the process wasn't agile at all**. It had none of the values that we've been talking about, till now. It followed the waterfall method, yes, and very safely, people would say that waterfall is not followed anymore. We all follow agile. But are we agile as people? As a society? That's the next level of introspection that hits us as conscious nations. These lessons learned are not only for one project but for all projects that involve waste of money. Look closer, it's lack of agility.

The Aftermath: The Healthcare.gov debacle resulted in significant reputational damage for the ACA and the Obama administration. It cost millions of dollars to fix the website and regain public trust. Check an excerpt from the report on Healthcare.gov, by the Office of Inspector General in Figure 2-9.

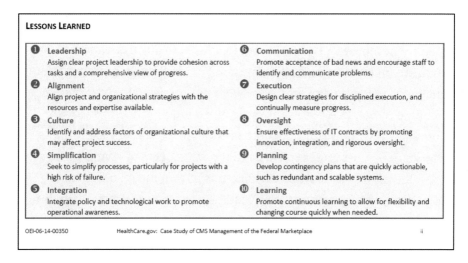

Figure 2-9. *From the Report on HealthCare.gov, USA, by the Office of Inspector General*

FBI Sentinel

We are talking of a time when big projects had failed because of traditional project management models, leading to losses in millions of dollars. Take the FBI Automated Case Support (ACS) system, built in the mid-1990s and was outdated and inadequate for the modern FBI. Well, outdated is a small word, considering that even in 2010, the FBI was dealing with reports on paper and extremely slow systems. The VCF system that was initiated to replace it could not be completed in 4 years of development, leading to a loss of 170 million dollars. The FBI Sentinel was funded by the Congress. A huge $351 million spent on it. Finally, when Agile experts were hired, outsourcing was cancelled, and a team of 40 developers finished the project in 1 year at a cost of 30 million dollars. The 9/11 committee rightly points out how the lack of organized data because of delayed deployment of an automated system played a part in the 9/11 attacks. Your systems need to be ready at the right time. Their production and output need to be accessible and relevant.

Fixing the FBI project was a huge task, but it required a strong mindset. What really changed? Jeff Johnson, in many places, quoted that he handled impediment removal. The team met regularly, to discuss impediments with the inspect and adapt cycle, and that led to flow. In previous attempts to make the software, the end users were not involved in interim demos. Jeff changed that. In a two-week cycle, the team planned to show an Increment – a working chunk of the product to a team of stakeholders. Demos in Jeff's own perspective were the key drivers of change. It brought trust in the entire team, where the client is part of the team. This was a huge jump from linear models. Needless to say, the Scrum Team did not only pay attention to the execution but adaptable habits as well. Continuous feedback from the stakeholders made the product better. They valued working software over comprehensive documentation. If you remember, we had marked this as a flaw of the linear model.

Not just the FBI project, all traditional projects had stacks of requirements, and every change was a contractual change. For such a project to be handed over was a nightmare. The Sentinel team under Jeff Johnson was tasked with brining up a working software. Requirements had to be prioritized and reprioritized after interim demos. Backlogs had to be refined. Hence, responding to change was much more important than following a plan. If you look through everything that was done to fix the project, it was introduction of agility – and not just a framework.

If you're interested in understanding in how Agile could help in turning around a $400M crisis, check out this video: https://youtu.be/P1YR9qe-fmk. It's an interview with Jeff himself, covering agile leadership, time to awareness as a key metric, and many other challenges that were overcome by a common-sense attitude that Jeff followed.

Boston's Big Dig Highway Project (1985–2006)

This tunnel and highway expansion project, originally budgeted at $2.5 billion, ballooned to a staggering $22 billion due to poor planning, scope creep, and delays caused by inflexible construction methods. Quality issues such as leaks, structural failures, and a fatal collapse added to the shame. You can always sit and make it sound intelligent and make charts and timelines and plans and try to stick to those plans, but what you'll not achieve is changing your habit. Becoming adaptive and agile to observe the changing demands of the project. The point of quoting such instances is not to glorify agile; it is to first point out the kind of money and effort that is going into projects with a fixated mindset and that too in vain.

Contrast this with a simple, effective case study for success in Scrum in the same industry: construction. McCarthy Building Companies adopted the Scrum framework, along with its philosophy, and three years on, they can successfully manage nine simultaneous projects. That's a 200–350% increase in productivity achieved with the same personnel.

There are many such case studies scattered on the world wide web, and if you put your mind to it, you'll understand that disasters happen when teams are not self-aware. Take this report for instance, for the F-35 Joint Strike Fighter. It shows you how and I quote, "Operational testing of the F-35 continues Reto be delayed—primarily by holdups in developing an aircraft simulator—even as DOD goes forward with the purchase of up to 152 aircraft a year. The more aircraft produced before testing is complete, the more it might cost to retrofit those aircraft if issues are discovered. We testified that if DOD moves forward as planned, it will have bought a third of all F-35s before determining that the aircraft is ready to move into full-rate production." This single line would tell you that the program has deeper issues. According to reports, the program aims to deliver over 3,000 F-35s in total, and as of November 2023, around 900 have been delivered. Deliveries are expected to continue until at least 2044.

As of 2023, the actual procurement costs for the F-35 program have already exceeded the initial estimates. The current estimates suggest a total procurement cost of approximately $414.5 billion.

To close this subsection, I'd like to take up a study in the success of Scrum. There are so many, but I had wanted to pick something the reader would not even think of. The author would leave it to the reader to take up more stories and make up their own mind, about when and how the world started changing with Scrum.

Scrum Goes As Far As Military Aviation

Gripen E: Scrum in Military Aviation

The Swedish Saab Gripen E program, utilizing Scrum methodology, offers a compelling case study of Agile practices in complex, high-stakes projects like military aviation. While attributing the Gripen E program's success solely to Scrum is inaccurate, here are some key takeaways from Mikael Sjoberg's book *Scrum in Military Aviation: Building a Jet Fighter with Scrum* (2019). They started small in 2010, gradually bringing more teams on board. Integrating different systems across teams proved tricky, and scaling Scrum within a large organization had its challenges. But there were wins too! Scrum fostered better teamwork and knowledge sharing, potentially leading to quicker problem-solving and potentially lower costs. The Gripen E's success likely involved more than just Scrum. Strong leadership, clear goals, and a supportive culture all played a part. It's safe to say that the umbrella of agile and lean thinking can be attributed to its success. But by adapting Scrum to their specific needs and tackling challenges head-on, the program offers valuable lessons for anyone considering Agile approaches in complex projects. "Owning the Sky with Agile" is another great report documented by Saab themselves. Even though, self-reported data should not be used to evaluate success or compare with competition, but it does go to show a lot of their values which they claimed to have shifted to as an organizational change. Throughout the report, they mention things like

- "...the autonomy to develop the best implementation for a particular local context."

- "3-week Sprint gives a pulse and rhythm to development."

- "Prioritization brings clarity on what should be done next."

- "The need for a strategic plan should however not be confused with a micromanaged Gantt-chart laying out detailed work for years to come."

- "Over the years Saab has evolved Retrospective to include not only the team perspective. There is also a Retrospective of Retrospectives, across teams. This is a scaled version to address feedback from the teams, common problems, and solutions, as well as leadership issues and management aspects from the Sprint."

- "Modularity of design allows modularity of organization."

- "Feedback is provided every sprint. Validation also takes place with pilots from the customers."

- "The goal is for every engineer, every day, to carry out the highest priority task with a minimum of obstacles."

What does this tell you? A conscious move toward agility, isn't it? The Swedish National Audit Office reports don't directly assess Agile practices, but they highlight the program's adherence to planned budgets and timelines, a potential indicator of efficient project management often associated with Agile principles. For example, the 2022 report "Uppföljning av anskaffningen av Gripen E" (Audit of the Gripen E procurement) acknowledges achieving cost targets.

Criticism of Scrum

All this is not to say that there are no challenges and criticism. Scrum is always easy to define and difficult to master and adopt. The discipline of Scrum is strict within the outer lightweight method. Also, many developers say the definition of Product Backlog could be more precise in the Scrum Guide. Simply saying that breaking it down does not help sometimes. Developers of Scrum started looking for ways of estimation, and techniques like story point estimation came up. Scaling Scrum is challenging, but a commitment to agile principles is what matters, and then, the framework is just a method that suits you. Tweak what you like, without compromising on principles.

Is Scrum Too Old for 2024?

The short answer is "No." Scrum cannot get old for any age I believe – because it's asking you to proceed step by step and check yourself at the end of every step. The philosophy is practical and full of self-awareness. For a detailed answer, follow my thought below.

Scrum implementation cannot be disregarded just because you don't understand its philosophy. In my personal experience, I find teams are still not agile enough. Upon deeper inspection, I realize that quarrels, job insecurities, and even corporate depression all happen because of lack of agility and can be attributed to deep-rooted issues such as socio-economic positioning of nations. You cannot expect people to be agile, where governments are radical. Not that you won't find agile people there, but by and large, people will inculcate habits of curbing dissent or not speaking up, of the governance sets that example for them.

I started my career in 2010, in a world where there was a one-line software requirement and no further requirements elicitation was taken from the client. Also, there were some projects where requirements went on endlessly without reaching implementation. A top-down approach toward a broken process and no addressal happened for what went wrong. Empiricism was totally defeated. Not spoken of. JIRA, Basecamp – these were mostly used as bug-tracking tools. User stories and epics were not used at all. The result was total chaos. Interim demos were rare and only to your manager. They were implemented through a rough plan, and no backlog was laid down. Sometimes, there would be projects where plans would be so detailed that there would be Gantt charts around them, without understanding the fact that software development cannot be predicted in advance. Requirements were exchanged through email and extended to developers, and they would give an estimate, again on email, and not even a testing buffer was included. (This challenge continues even now, by the way.) This was simply because a requirement wasn't inspected. In years to come, my interviewers would ask me if I had implemented agile methods in my projects, and I would say no – the reason being my previous employers had limited exposure to agile. I remember I spoke of behavior-driven development wherever I went, and very few companies I have worked with have made conscious efforts to even pen down acceptance criteria along with user stories.

The pertinent question: Is this book required in 2024? Yes, very much. The world we live in is broken. To bring values into it requires a social change. Call that change anything you want, but change will remain a constant. A world of continuous learning and empiricism is what you want, not fixated structures that might become shackles later.

Kanban

The next popular approach is the Kanban visualization, based on the Just in Time production at Toyota. It should not be treated as a process, however. Kanban can be combined with Scrum very neatly, or it can be independent of Scrum – and in that respect, it should be treated as a visualization method only. The thought behind it, however, is far more important. There might be a lot of language around Kanban and Lean, but the core remains avoiding waste. Before we delve into its history, which would be found in many other books, let's take an aside, and talk about three simple examples of waste in today's world:

- **Food Waste:** Globally, one-third of all food produced goes uneaten, amounting billions of tons annually. This "waste mountain" has devastating consequences, from resource depletion to greenhouse gas emissions.

- **Energy Waste:** The Global Alliance for Buildings and Construction (GABC) estimates that buildings alone account for 30% of global energy consumption, often due to outdated infrastructure and practices. This highlights the need for improved energy management to reduce national account waste.

- **Healthcare Waste:** The World Health Organization (WHO) reports that healthcare facilities generate significant waste, including unused medication, medical equipment, and hazardous materials. Improper disposal of this waste poses health and environmental risks.

Give a pause here, and ask how you can eliminate or minimize such waste. Identifying waste in regular life is an important precursor to understanding Lean. Just like agility in real life is taken to the workspace, so is Lean. In the next chapter, we delve into identifying waste around us, in our personal lives and professions.

For now, the single thought that should awaken anyone who is still witnessing waste – the thought of waste being a social crime. This thought was not only resounded by Taiichi Ohno in his book, *Toyota Production*

System: Beyond Large-Scale Production but has been very consciously raised by many leaders of nations in the world. Spiritually aware national leaders have been able to handle hard crises by avoiding waste and even vanity and respecting the need of a nation, in contrast to leaders who have led their nations to disaster and hunger crises by not focusing on sustainability. How does all of this preaching useful to Kanban, you ask? Well, everyone knows now, and if you see waste, it's lack of poor governance. We'll see in a moment how Kanban can and has helped in all such examples. First, let's define Kanban for the benefit of readers who are unaware of it.

Welcome to the philosophy of Kanban, a visual method born from the chaos of Toyota's manufacturing lines in the 1940s. Inspired by Kanban, meaning "signboard" in Japanese, this system revolutionized production by focusing on visualizing tasks, limiting work in progress, and driving continuous improvement. Teams visualize their work on boards, using cards to represent tasks. By limiting the number of "WIP" tasks, bottlenecks are exposed, and focus is maximized. Transparency reigns, as everyone sees the workflow and can collaborate proactively. The Kanban philosophy is simple yet profound: respect for people, continuous learning, and adaptability. Its visual display is simple too – a column each for tasks categorized as **To Do**, **In Progress**, **In Review**, and **Done**. You can play with the categories as you wish, and these are nothing but the status of where a task in the pipeline lies. Essentially, these are the most important statuses that impact production. I personally find two more status columns very useful: "Blocked" and "Sent for User Acceptance." People do split Done into QA Sign Off and Production Sign Off, but that is how your process is staged. Essentially, what you are doing is just in time manufacturing, because you are pulling as much as you can take, finishing it, and pushing it to the next person in line. The core principles are as follows and are actually the principles of lean (although the philosophy is bigger):

1. **Visualize Work:** This fundamental principle emphasizes making work visible to everyone involved. This is typically achieved through Kanban boards with columns representing different stages of work (e.g., To Do, In Progress, Done) and cards representing individual tasks. Visualizing work **fosters transparency**, allows for better collaboration, and helps identify bottlenecks.

2. **Limit Work in Progress (WIP):** This principle encourages focusing on finishing tasks before starting new ones. By setting WIP limits for each stage of the process, you prevent overloading and ensure smooth flow. This improves lead times, reduces context switching, and allows for better focus on quality. For instance, on one of my projects, our team decided that in one day of allocated time for a project, we would keep only three tasks per developer, every task being allowed to span only for an hour. That way, every software developer would work for three hours of the allocated five and test his work for two hours. Such a decision can be arrived at by the team itself. **We eliminated waste** by picking up tasks that we could finish. And trust me, every principle of Lean rests on the basic pillar of avoiding waste.

3. **Flow Optimization:** Kanban emphasizes continuous improvement of the workflow. By **analyzing bottlenecks**, visualizing dependencies, and adapting the process based on real-time data, you can streamline work and make it flow more efficiently. This involves encouraging collaboration,

removing non-value-adding activities, and constantly seeking better ways to work. Again, for an example, there are boards with columns specifically for blockers. There are facilitation techniques which would identify blockers of the day and identify removal procedures before beginning the next set of tasks. Another analogy that I can think of is from the education sector. The carry over system allows students with failed courses to accumulate them as "carry overs" and clear them at their convenience within a stipulated time frame. This system often carries stricter limitations on the duration allowed to clear outstanding courses but does not hinder year progression. What have we achieved here? Flow. We haven't allowed one blocker to become a dependency on other aspects of learning, but we have addressed a neat way of handling the impediment itself. Compare this with the traditional way of retaining students in a class failing the entire program or grade. This led to less change in organizational structure but sadly affected students psychologically. The reason I pulled up this analogy was because it will help us as a society to observe such principles and avoid blockages in each other's way, reducing dependencies.

4. **Pull Systems:** Unlike traditional push systems where work is assigned regardless of capacity, Kanban utilizes pull systems. Teams only pull new work when they have the capacity to start it, based on downstream demand. This prevents overburdening and ensures **focus on tasks with immediate value**.

Case Study in Lean and Kanban

Cleveland Clinic, Ohio

Here, we quickly look at how it was with Lean thinking and an efficient cross-functional team that Cleveland Clinic was able to reduce outpatient chemotherapy wait times from an average of 60 minutes to 20 minutes. (Read more: Lean Enterprise Institute). Think of what that means to the patient. Think of what value that adds to the professional goal.

The article cited above is filled with examples where benefits of lean management, daily huddles, and impediment removal are discussed with quantifiable results. It speaks of visual management tools to understand the status of operations in an area.

Another study recommended to learners for Lean is the study of Toyota. While the lessons are many, you could quickly glance at The Wiki Entry for The Toyota Production System. Two noteworthy mentions here: identifying waste, which we take up in the next chapter, and the Andon cord. The **Andon Cord** is a key concept in **Lean manufacturing**, particularly in the Toyota Production System (TPS). It is a visual or physical signaling system that allows workers to stop the production line when they detect a problem, such as a defect, safety issue, or process error. The Andon Cord empowers employees to take immediate action to address issues, ensuring that quality is prioritized over production speed. **Problem Alerts** bring up anomalies immediately, including machine downtime, quality issues, tooling malfunctions, operator delays, and material shortages. This swift notification allows for prompt corrective action. Picture a factory buzzing with activity, and overhead hangs a digital "lamp" – the Andon. Each station is assigned a number on this board. If a machine hiccups, a sensor triggers its number to light up. Operators can also pull a cord, illuminating their number for assistance. This "flash" instantly alerts the team leader, and colored lights on machines (red for issues, green for smooth sailing) provide further visual cues. This simple yet powerful tool ensures problems are seen, addressed swiftly, and quality never compromised. The tool was a direct enabler for visualization of work and flow optimization. The article also describes the cultural change that brought about measurable success.

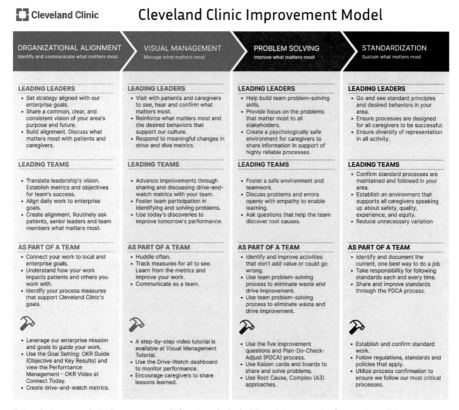

The image has been recreated using the exact same text and information on the Cleveland Clinic Website. No Copyright Infringement is intended.

© Cleveland Clinic Foundation 2021

Figure 2-10. *The Cleveland Clinic Improvement Model*
Image source: Cleveland Clinic Website

Learning from history is the best way to understand the importance of what you're doing and how you can do it better. I had somewhere asked the reader to map the thought behind the process. Figure 2-11 provides a map for values in popular methodologies that I made for myself:

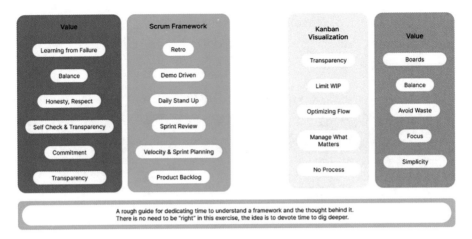

Figure 2-11. *Values Behind Frameworks*

Summary

This chapter does not seek to replace a course – it is merely a historic walkthrough of events of how thought process behind management changed over time. In the next chapter, we combine Agile with Lean and many more innovative practices.

Further Reading

https://www.planet-lean.com/articles/jeff-sutherland-scrum-interview

https://openviewpartners.com/blog/an-overview-of-the-burndown-chart-and-its-history/

https://newbo.co/scrum-fighter-planes/

https://www.goodreads.com/en/book/show/113086

https://www.atlassian.com/agile/scrum

https://www.scruminc.com/scrum-hardware-full-scale-manufacturing/

https://www.lean.org/the-lean-post/articles/from-cradle-to-gate-to-cradle-to-cradle-a-lean-approach-to-sustainable-product-design/

https://agilemanifesto.org/principles.html

Exercise

Stop creating to-do lists for some time. At the end of the day, just write down what you accomplished, and be at peace with it. The mind, outside of the workplace, can sometimes create unnecessary pressure with a hundred things to be done the next day. Take life smoothly and not in a race. Discipline is a slow process, and nobody is judging anyone.

CHAPTER 3

The Lean Mindset and Innovative Agile Practices

We've already delved into popular Agile methods and their forerunners, recognizing that values are the true north star, not the specific framework. It's the people who matter most, and forcing Agile onto them won't work. Instead, we need to help them understand the value Agile offers over their existing approach, encouraging them to retain the useful aspects of their current system while gradually integrating Agile principles. Most importantly, this chapter focuses on cultivating a lean mindset, a crucial step before customizing Agile. Remember, Agile should not deviate from its core principles. In the pursuit of "agility," we can't simply allow people to do whatever they please. Agile serves as a guiding star, not a free-for-all. After preparing the ground, we talk of innovation in agile so that we can continue to understand how flexible we all are without compromising on our values.

Lean

Forget dry, corporate case studies for a minute. This is about you, about making your life better. Think of Lean as a toolkit for personal optimization, not just corporate efficiency. Imagine walking into a

© Kanika Sud 2025
K. Sud, *Customizable Agile Development*, https://doi.org/10.1007/979-8-8688-1055-8_3

cluttered room, tripping over unused items, struggling to find what you need. And trust me, if you're the right kind of disorganized, you can trip over dust in your own room, not just things! Then, picture transforming that space: decluttering, organizing, maximizing useable area. This, in essence, is the Lean mindset: identifying and eliminating waste to optimize value. But its impact extends far beyond tidying up a physical space – it touches our daily lives, organizations, and even governments.

From my own life, my father gave me a simple tip which I never obeyed till I had to manage my own home. He told me that everything should have a specific place in the house; don't let that go astray. Not that you must kill if something is out of place, but keeping it in the same place, after having used it, was *his* way to run into ways of avoiding clutter. You can write books about it, but there was a generation that knew this, because their lives were simple. They knew how to not waste time in domestic and outdoor activities, and they carried the same culture in their workspaces. My mother always told me to measure my output during a day, after I passed college and was still looking for a job, so that I could avoid getting lethargic. Now these days, her daughter writes books about end of day status updates! Again, it's not that inspection and adaptation can be attributed to a modern age consciousness. Obviously not. It's just that modern order made us forget what we already knew in different aspects of life. Reminding ourselves of these sides of life is not revolutionary – it is a favor to ourselves.

Lean has quantified results just like Scrum. We'll give you facts and you can go digging. General Electric saved billions through Lean, with lead times reduced by a whopping 80%. Imagine shaving months off a project! Efficiency translates to financial gains. Henry Ford Health System reduced patient wait times in emergency rooms by 50%. Lean saves lives by improving healthcare delivery. The state of Kentucky streamlined government processes, saving taxpayers over $1 billion. Efficiency basically was seen through the lens of lesser wastage. All principles that we mentioned in the previous chapter are closely related to finding value and **avoiding waste**.

For best results of fusing Agile and Lean, we need to understand that Lean is the foundation of Agile. Lean is a management philosophy that helps teams make better decisions about how to invest their time, energy, and money. And it is much bigger than what we discussed in the previous chapter. Here, we shall take a deep dive into identifying waste.

Identifying Waste

For avoiding waste, we need to first identify waste. While the previous chapter touched on *examples* of waste, this chapter makes you reason with yourself to see if something is wasting your time and energy and consequently your money.

From the book, *Lean Software Development: An Agile Toolkit: An Agile Toolkit (Agile Software Development Series)* by Mary Poppendieck and Tom Poppendieck, some awesome excerpts from the first chapter lead to a lot of understanding about waste. We shall borrow heavily from those excerpts and build our own opinion on them as well, with experiences from our daily corporate lives. The first chapter in the book mentioned above shows the following table, detailing the seven wastes of manufacturing and software development. See Figure 3-1 for more details.

The Seven Wastes of Manufacturing	The Seven Wastes of Software Development
Inventory	Partially Done Work
Extra Processing	Extra Processes
Overproduction	Extra Features
Transportation	Task Switching
Waiting	Waiting
Motion	Motion
Defects	Defects

Figure 3-1. *Identifying Categories of Waste by Mary Poppendieck and Tom Poppendieck*

We choose not to describe what Mary and Tom have already described in their book, i.e., on the right-hand side. The terms are self-descriptive. In Chapter 5, we give you plenty of scenarios, which relate with these kinds of waste. However, in addition to the seven categories of waste pointed out by Mary and Tom Poppendieck, we seek to introduce a few more, which might shed light on how time's getting wasted. (Again, like the seven pointed out by the esteemed authors mentioned above, these six are interlinked as well.)

1. Lack of standardization

2. Underutilization of talent

3. Complexities of distributed teams

4. Generalization vs. specialization

5. Weak estimation, overestimation, and planning horrors

The reader might even feel that these categories fade into what has already been mentioned in the seven primary categories, but I would encourage teams to categorize kinds of waste regularly. Let's see how these five above lead to waste.

Also, our point is that these waste categories and more can be related with any industry and not just software and manufacturing. The idea of what adds value and what does not, needs to be looked into regularly, for any industry. I shall first restrict myself to examples in daily life. For instance, when dad told us to replace whatever we've used at the very same place, he wanted us to stop wasting time the next time we needed it. That implicitly happened because of the **lack of standardization**. Now, if you maintain the same place for your stationery in the house, you'll look for it in the same place every time. There are things that can benefit from standardization, and identifying them at work is easier if you inculcate the habit of doing things that way in life. The same can be observed **for ambiguous requirements, unused features, and so many more categories**. Now, try and map this to your chosen industry. I would strongly encourage you to do this exercise for multiple industries. I can give you a lead, and leave you to it. I've mapped it for software and for construction and for regular life in Figure 3-2.

Construction	Software	Daily Life
Incomplete specifications (e.g., missing details about materials or dimensions)	**Insufficient user research** (e.g., not understanding user needs)	**Assumptions** (e.g., assuming someone knows what you mean)
Lack of consensus (e.g., disagreement among stakeholders about the design)	**Conflicting stakeholder expectations** (e.g., different departments with conflicting goals)	**Misaligned goals** (e.g., Having no agenda)
Change Management (e.g, changes due to supply chain problems, unexpected site conditions etc.)	**Scope Creep** (e.g, Clients taking agility for granted and changing requirements more often than possible)	**Life being Life!** You know when things can really shock you from all directions. Your mind cannot, at that moment, sort out what needs to be worked on next.

Figure 3-2. *Ambiguous Requirements: Software vs. Construction*

Lack of Standardization

I'll now add a few anecdotes of waste in software development that hindered productivity in my own years of experience. I've just spent a little over a decade in this industry, and there is so much more to learn, but when I read about visionaries, the one thing that fascinates me is how relatable they are. The first example I'd like to quote here is about quality assurance. I remember companies where the quality assurance team along with managers would not prioritize bugs into high, medium, and low. Forget that, I've seen QA team leads writing on JIRA, "As discussed on call, the attached video is not working right." An honest resource assessment for such team leads would not be done. The bug description suffered immensely, and not even three fields were provided: expected results, actual results, and steps to reproduce. For churning out profits or avoiding hiring trouble, just any kind of resources were hired, leave alone "motivated individuals." The quality analyst would pile up bugs without relevance. The resulting system was a chaos and a faulty build that would not be worthy of customer use. When I read the Healthcare.gov case study many many years later, I realized that the scale of such waste and the way you address it causes havoc at all levels.

In Figure 3-3, I give a simple image giving an example of how to avoid waste in quality assurance. It's just a first step. Nothing fancy. Yet, it makes a huge impact. And it's out of experience that I say that nine out of ten members of quality assurance did not submit adequate information on bugs. Many leaders thought that testing was not required and developers should do it themselves. I remember a QA lead of nine years of experience was hell-bent on not writing the steps to reproduce the bug. I just asked for a good bug description, but no, it simply wouldn't digest. You meet people of all kinds, and there is a way to make them understand. Meanwhile, let us get back to the example in Figure 3-3.

Small Steps to Improve Quality Assurance

BAD BUG DESCRIPTION
Causes Back and Forth iterations and lack of understanding

GOOD BUG DESCRIPTION
Avoids Waste Of Time and Energy

BADLY WRITTEN

The app keeps crashing on my phone.

PROBLEMS WITH THIS BUG

- What is the specific model of your phone?
- What operating system version are you using?
- Can you describe the exact steps you took to encounter the crash?
- What were you doing in the app before the crash occurred?
- Is there any error message or other information that appears on the screen?
- What is the expected result? Without crashing, should it lead somewhere?
- No suggestion provided about crash analytics integration
- Visual screenshots or videos need to be provided as evidence, if possible.

FORMAT EXPECTED

- Bug Title
- Steps To Reproduce
- Actual Result
- Expected Result
- Is there any error message or other information that appears on the screen?
- Suggestions and Improvements can be given as well.

Shows lack of standardization - and this leads to waste because of lack of clarity.

WELL WRITTEN

A clearly written bug with clear and concise information about the problem, making it easier for developers to understand and fix. As a bare minimum, it should answer the questions listed under "Problems" without developers having to ask for it.

BUG TITLE

"App Crashes on Home Screen"

STEPS TO REPRODUCE

- Open the app.
- Tap on the "Home" button.
- The app crashes immediately.
- Video Attached

DEVICE & OS INFO

- Phone Model: iPhone 14 Pro
- Operating System: iOS 17.1
- App Version: 2.3.1

EXPECTED RESULT

The app should display the home screen content.

ACTUAL RESULT

The app crashes with the error message: "Unfortunately, App has stopped."

SUGGESTIONS

The system should allow developers to analyze crash trends, identify common patterns, and prioritize bug fixes.

Avoids waste, increases productivity

Figure 3-3. *Standardization of Bug Description and Its Impact on Waste*

If you notice carefully, the lack of standardization is a clear indication of waste. Apply it to your profession, and you'll get tons of scenarios where you experience such a case.

Underutilization of Talent

Not fully utilizing the skills and capabilities of employees, leading to reduced productivity and job dissatisfaction. It's the same thing if you force fit a person into a role he is not meant for or if a useful resource is lying idle and underutilized. I've seen an extremely messed up system where a lady I knew had the potential to lead quality assurance and was certified to do it. She had the relevant experience too, but just because her senior manager did not approve of it, the quality assurance team kept reporting to someone who was just not meant for thc job. This colleague of mine also had the potential to set a process as an agile coach, but the Founder did not take any solution seriously. Ineffective resource allocation, the lack of a challenging project, and other similar factors led to complete loss of drive and motivation even among the best in that place. Yet, another case was when a young aspiring Android Developer wanted to work on AI. The company took a straightforward viable decision that since his cost to the company was low and could be used for multiple Android projects, the most natural way of utilizing him was to allocate him on as many Android projects as possible. Believe me, the developer begged for an opportunity in AI and even said that he would make a research project in AI. No, the leadership team would not have it. They gave it to an interested resource, who added no value to it. Result? The Android developer left the company and is continuing developing his own apps, freelancing into AI opportunities. He was the best I had worked with, and to lose him was the biggest example of a company not being able to understand where talent lies.

It is to be mentioned that some people have completely twisted this principle to suit their cost needs. When they feel that they can no longer utilize an employee, he is laid off - even without notice and within months of hiring, by saying that it is his problem. Neither can you hire to fire nor can you pass on the blame for not having work. The underlying ethic of honesty to yourself is bigger than the outcome of anything.

Complexity Due to Distributed Teams

Distributed teams, while offering flexibility, introduce complexities that can lead to project waste. Time zone differences, the lack of real-time collaboration, delayed responses, weak team cohesion, and the lack of spontaneity in problem-solving might be some of the cases that leaders will speak about when talking of problems due to distributed teams and remote working culture. Some leaders, however, can manage a great output even with such teams, and some can't. Depends on how patient and honest you are. Depends on how you carry such situations. Irrespective of the rule book, there are things that you learn with experience, and no guide out there can tell you what to do. Guides might point you to tools, video calls, and the like – but managing remote teams comes with a knack for doing it and an awareness of whether or not you can do it at all. It varies from leader to leader, and hence as professionals, being cautious of the waste that such remote teams are creating is something that we might want to look into.

I remember working in a team of ten people for a mind wellness app. The client chose the iOS developer from the United States because he was based out of the United States. For cost reasons, the US clients outsourced Android apps to developers and a Scrum Master in India. For reasons unknown, the Product Owner was based out of China. There were two testers. The one based out of India tested the APIs and the front end. The one based out of the United States tested the iOS app. The Scrum Master was **nonbillable** so she was asked to give two hours a day only. Yes. Welcome to the world of service-based startups in India. I found it a strange mix, but the result was not strange – it was predictable. The efforts that went into managing in different time zones, making similar components for both platforms, reviewing code quality, and explaining context of the market involved, hellholes of code and bugs, and everything else about the app were simply adding to waste. The iOS app was never completely in sync with the Android app. We had one-week Sprints. I suggested adding keeping the entire team based out of one time zone, but the client would not have it. With extreme struggles and perseverance, we reached a velocity of 100%, but the client still found issues where she would not agree with the delivery of one component or the other. The team would just not come on the same call, leave alone co-location.

Generalization vs. Specialization

Then, there is another common scenario where generalists and specialists are mixed up in a company and employees are made to feel that they do not understand business outcomes, whereas the real root cause is that generalists are placed in a role made for specialists. Generalists, with broad knowledge and skills, can adapt to changing circumstances and contribute to diverse tasks. However, they may lack deep expertise, leading to suboptimal solutions and increased project timelines. Specialists, on the other hand, possess in-depth knowledge in specific areas, ensuring high-quality work. Yet, they may be less flexible and unable to handle unexpected challenges. Sometimes, people come from a product-driven background and placed as functional leads in multiple projects at the same time, which leads to their irritation, the lack of scaling horizontally, and not being able to understand what to do in such cases. Small organizations hire people for profits. That's the core of their work culture, irrespective of what they say. And identifying whether a person is really fit for the role vs. closing an open position isn't even on the table. This circus, as I choose to call it, leads to more waste than imaginable. More cautious hiring and keeping deliverables and quality in mind are just some of the ways of understanding how to utilize talent in your own company. Besides, if you are growing, identifying who fits what opportunity is essential for you to stand out as an employer. To balance these complexities, organizations should carefully assess project requirements and allocate resources accordingly. A hybrid approach, combining generalists and specialists, can optimize project outcomes. For instance, a generalist project manager can oversee the overall project, while specialists handle specific technical tasks. By understanding the strengths and limitations of each role and each individual, organizations can avoid the pitfalls of overgeneralization or overspecialization, ultimately preventing waste and ensuring project success. It is a very slow process, but it is not something we can ignore.

Weak Estimation, Overestimation, and Planning Horrors

I've seen developers who would flatly say, "You can forward four hours per API as the estimate!" – that's it. As a Product Owner, it shocked me to even absorb that people do not want to breakdown a task at all before estimating it. But those are extreme cases. There are people who make a sincere effort at estimation and fail at it. Anyone who has been a developer or has been into a coding hell knows how his estimates can become a joke over the life cycle of a project.

Refer to Figure 2-7 for the road map we showed you, and notice that the road map just shows features and which Sprint it will be delivered. The breakdown of the features into user stories is done by the Product Owner, and the breakdown of a user story into subtasks comes from the developers (the execution team) itself. So where do estimations go wrong? While Scrum does not hard press on how to break down work structure, it remains a fact that until your work is broken down into good subtasks by the Scrum Team, the estimations of the Scrum Team will not be accurate. So, does that mean the Work Breakdown Structure needs a separate inspection during Scrum before we conclude our estimates? And by whom? I seek to answer these questions in my own framework, in

Chapter 6. For now, I'll leave you with the thought that extremely detailed planning and extremely vague planning both cause waste. And both are paths to avoid.

Before closing the section on identifying waste, I'd like to mention what Dan Norman said in his book *Design for a Better World*:

> *People have naturally evolved to seek meaning and explanation, yet we are forced to live in a world where meaning is buried beneath documents and pronouncements that use abstract and complex specialized terminology - legalistic, technical, and governmental.*

> —Dan Norman

You get your facts right when you eliminate waste in your work.

Innovation Through Facilitation and Team Structure

Through Meetings

The art of facilitating cannot be ignored in any discussion on innovation industry frameworks. It is through conversation that most innovation is initiated unless you're a researcher who is working alone. Here, instead of preaching, we introduce tried and tested tips and tricks which really help in improving performance, in many different industries. Below are basic teasers of how I tried to add color and empathy to standups, meetings in agile execution. I've also added a few examples of team structures that worked for me and for industry professionals. The mind is the limit, and my intention is only to encourage practitioners to use facilitation and alternate team topologies as a powerful technique for innovation.

Hot Seat Rotation

Back in 2017, we were working on a polling app, and one day, chaos hit, one day after the launch. Users started reporting that the social media login feature wasn't working. It was a critical feature – without it, engagement dropped, and we couldn't afford that. The worst part? The developer and tester who originally set up the login integration had left the company, and there was no documentation to guide us. It was one of those moments where the air in the room felt heavy. I was on a call with the client, who was obviously shouting. That day, one of our Android developers took the hot seat – not because it was her responsibility, but because she was not afraid of the hot seat (as we called it later). This wasn't about assigning blame. It was about ownership. She kicked things off calmly. "The error logs point to an issue with the OAuth token retrieval," she said. "But everything seems normal at first glance." She had already checked the API keys, and they were valid. Our front-end lead chimed in: "The UI hasn't changed. Could it be a third-party API issue?" "No, but the callback URL looks suspicious." That got everyone's attention. She noticed it didn't match the URL registered with the social media provider. The DevOps engineer immediately added, "Let's check the deployment logs – maybe an environment variable wasn't updated." And that's when it clicked. We dug into the code and found a hard-coded callback URL – an old one that hadn't been updated when we changed environments. It was a relic from the previous developer, a line of code that should have been dynamic but wasn't. "We need to replace the hard-coded URL with the correct environment variable," someone said from the team. Within hours, we pushed the fix to staging, tested it, and rolled it out. The issue was resolved, and the app's login feature was back online. Looking back, that moment was a testament to how initiative and ownership can transform a crisis into a shared victory. No blame, just problem-solving – and it all started with someone stepping into the hot seat.

We fondly called it the hot seat practice after that, and I have implemented it in many projects, especially which are cross-platform, or where everyone might not be aware of legacy systems, or people might not be on the same page for whatever reason. Making one person speak about the issue has helped me understand how cross-functional the team member really is.

The concept of distributed ownership in agile has always brought questions. Nobody wants the single-ended accountability for product health, not even a Product Owner – who is in effect answerable for the defects, bugs, working condition, and justifications. By product health, we mean how fit the product is according to the committed delivery. So, what do we do? Hot seat rotation in meetings is one way which allows people to rotate ownership in something that we all run from. Bugs. Whatever the bug might be, in whatever component of the app or hardware, the person on the hot seat today should be able to speak about it, work toward a root cause analysis, and contribute toward it's solving. This one thing fosters ways of bug solving that many don't admit, and trust me, it will make everybody a natural at taking ownership, when they realize that it's not just someone's mistake – it's the product that needs to be corrected.

Role Play: Who Is the Client Today?

I've tried this one many a time. It's a great exercise in playing the turn coat or the devil's advocate. One member from my Daily Standups would be asked to play the client. That person would not be the Scrum Master, the Product Owner, or any managerial role. In a Scrum Team, such a person would come from the Scrum development team. This had multifaceted benefits. It made the standup change for at least one day a week. The client would just think in terms of business, and that would make the developer walk out of his tech role. Developers would realize the Product Owner's responsibility, and that led to more responsible work from the team. Think of this as a business-centric perspective, but with a "Client in the Room" approach. Be mindful that prioritizing the "client" perspective doesn't overshadow technical discussions and problem-solving, and neither should it create unnecessary pressure or undermine the Product Owner's authority. We've tried doing it by encouraging the "client" to ask questions from a business perspective, not by dictating solutions. You can also consider a time limit for the "client" segment, instead of changing the whole decorum of the client standup meeting.

Note   It is to be noted that this "client" is not the customer. The end customer's empathy map is laid down in persona-specific meetings and is described next in the "Product over Project Meeting" section.

In one of our projects – a winery management app – we elevated the "Client in the Room" approach to new heights. Each Sprint, a different developer played the role of the client during one of our standups. Let me share a pivotal moment from one such Sprint.

The challenge was clear: The client's end customer refused to release their historical data, yet the entire use case hinged on it. We were stuck in a deadlock. During one standup, Bharat, our Android developer, stepped into the client role and framed the problem bluntly:"What happens if we don't get the historical data in time? What's the potential loss if we delay the app's launch?"

The team leaned in as Hiten, a front-end engineer, responded, "How will we create before-and-after graphs to show how frontline workers improved when they were trained using this app? Those visuals are critical for the app." His work on the data-binding consoles made the lack of historical information feel like a major setback.

Bharat, embodying the client, replied, "Their data is locked under tight restrictions, and they're not likely to release it anytime soon. What's the alternative?"

Another developer jumped in: "What if we focus on areas that don't depend on historical data? The Trivia and raffle features, for example, or the entire video content section for marketing. These are independent of past data."

Bharat nodded thoughtfully. "That's a solid pivot."

And just like that, our MVP took shape. We shifted focus to the data-independent features, which enabled us to launch on schedule. Over time, this approach became the foundation for a SaaS product that we scaled across multiple verticals. The reusable, data-independent modules were tailored for different clients, while the data-dependent sections were customized as needed.

This experience demonstrated the value of stepping into the client's shoes. It fostered innovative thinking, turning a potential roadblock into a strategic advantage, and ultimately shaped the product's success.

In similar meetings, that followed, the *dummy client* would:

1. **Adjust Business Alignment:** Developers were reminded of the bigger picture – meeting business commitments not just building cool features.

2. **Handle Backlog Prioritization:** This was very useful, when we tried to prioritize the backlog. When one person was delegated as a client, prioritization became a lot simpler, and there was more aid to the Product Owner for the activity.

3. **Encourage Cross-Role Empathy:** Developers gained insight into the pressures the Product Owner and client face, fostering more thoughtful collaboration.

4. **Question the ROI:** "Which features will bring the quickest ROI?" "Are there any high-impact features that can be delivered with minimal effort?" – These were questions that the team began to ask regularly, contributing to scope and becoming truly autonomous.

We often teased Bharat about being the client, but once every Sprint, we intentionally brought the "client" into the room for various purposes – even for something as straightforward as an audit. It was a fabulous team I worked with, something I'll never forget, because within that team space, we created something bigger, something better – an environment for product thinking and growth.

Product over Project Meeting

This is an extension of the client role-play meeting. Here, the client is the customer.

Product over Project is a concept discussed in *The Lean Mindset: Ask the Right Questions* by Mary and Tom Poppendieck. After all, we live in a world where it's easy to lose sight of what we are making among stakeholder desires, contract limitations, human factors, errors of omission, and commission.

The main emphasis of this kind of meeting would be to realign the trajectory of the product toward its purpose and utility for the end customer. This time, keep the customer in the room. Such meetings can be dedicated to personas, competitors, market segments, and the like. This meeting is nothing about timelines or achievements. It is more about how the product should work for the end customer. Be cautious that you should not let the team become a feature factory, because simply introducing multiple features in the name of Product over Project is not the goal. You cannot lose sight of what you have committed, but you need to realign yourselves and see if what you've made is going in the larger scheme of things. We hope the following episode puts things into light.

In the context of the same winery management app, we had a feature for wine tasting notes, whereby frontline managers would take notes for wine tasting, and that would help them encourage club members to retain their memberships through better information about the wines, etc. We realized the value of occasionally stepping away from the usual Scrum dynamics to reset our product thinking. We had been so immersed in the details of timelines, feature deliveries, and technical constraints that we needed a moment to pause and rethink the purpose and utility of the app for the end user.

Gagan, who was focused on Android issues at the time, suddenly raised a thought as he was reviewing the home screen of the wine tasting notes section:"How do we blend wines?"This seemingly simple question triggered a whole new level of discussion. It was one of those rare moments when a team member's curiosity led to a deeper dive into the product's core purpose. Gagan wasn't asking a technical question; he was questioning the very nature of the product itself.

The team paused, and what followed was a discussion about how the app should actually present the wine blending process. Was it just a static set of wine tasting notes, or should it communicate the blending process to users in a way that felt interactive and informative?

This led to a complete rethinking of the information architecture of the app. Instead of simply displaying tasting notes as a static list, we began brainstorming ways to represent the blending process visually – could we show the different types of grapes, the proportions, or perhaps even the process itself in a step-by-step guide for the user?

Chakshu suggested that the app should visually represent wine blends, showing how different wines come together to create a unique flavor profile.

Anima proposed adding interactive elements like ingredient tool tips that users could hover over to learn more about each component of the blend, helping them understand the decisions behind the product. She even added an animation that would make blending seem interesting and highlighted the activity as the major verb on the screen.

Finally, we discussed creating a timeline of the wine blending and aging process, allowing users to explore the wine's journey from grape to glass, and how the trivia questions should add weight to such questions apart from the rest.

What started as a simple query about blending wines transformed into a complete overhaul of how we approached **user interaction** within the app. The feature was no longer just a list of wine tasting notes – it became an interactive, engaging experience that provided users with deeper insights into the process.

The client was extremely impressed on how we pitched the story to him that day. I still remember the team that was so proud of itself, but the only factor that had weighed in was empathy toward the end customer.

Role Play: Who Is the Scrum Master Today: Rotating the Scrum Master role, especially assigning it to junior or quieter team members, can reveal hidden strengths and fresh perspectives. Rajesh, typically quiet during meetings, showcased a unique approach by restructuring the standup to focus on prioritizing blockers rather than status updates.

Similarly, Lakshman's approach, where the standup concluded in five minutes, adhered to industry standard expectations by focusing on brief status updates and action items. This contrast highlights how varying facilitation methods can serve different purposes – whether focusing on swift updates or in-depth problem resolution.

Key Takeaways:

1. **Encouraging Participation:** Allowing juniors to lead can boost confidence and reveal innovative problem-solving methods.

2. **Adaptability in Facilitation:** Different facilitators bring diverse styles – some prioritize in-depth discussions; others focus on efficiency.

3. **Team Dynamics Awareness:** Understanding who is open to change and who prefers structure is crucial for effective facilitation.

During one Sprint, Bharat, our diligent Android developer, took on the role of Scrum Master. Known for his people management skills, one day he steered the call as a **"Focus Mode" Connect with API Design Emphasis.** He had noticed consistent problems in APIs. Bharat highlighted a key issue: inconsistent data formats between the API responses and what the Android app expected. He invited Gagan, to discuss. Together, they mapped out critical API endpoints that needed refinement and prioritized setting up a joint design call. This was further discussed with Vishal, our back-end developer. The beauty of this call was that I did nothing, it was an initiative by the team, for the team and the product, I was truly an observer, and whether the APIs were consistent after that or not, I saw a people-leader emerging, who could bind them together, making them think critically.

Innovation Sprints

Give your team research labs. And this lab can be of any type. One example could come directly from digging the lessons learnt in other projects or even the tasks you came across while completing the previous project. At the time of execution, maybe you took the next best approach, but now if some of your team has the time, build pluggable solutions with alternative approaches. Give yourselves repeated labs to think it through. Product companies already have this approach since they cannot thrive without ideation labs. It's time the service sector adopts such research too.

Once, we were tasked with improving the user experience when uploading images to the app. The initial implementation simply allowed users to select images, but we realized that many images needed to be cropped to fit specific dimensions. Instead of rushing to implement this feature as part of the main Sprint, we created a research lab session where the team could explore different cropping libraries and approaches.

One of our developers suggested using a cropping library that would allow users to crop images directly in the app before uploading them. This would save time for the users and streamline the process, preventing the need for post-upload cropping. We tested several cropping solutions

74

and decided on one that was simple, efficient, and easy to integrate into our app. By setting up a dedicated research session, we ensured that the cropping feature wasn't just a quick fix but a well-thought-out enhancement that improved the overall user experience.

A good example of this was during the development of an iOS app, which turned out to be more complex than its Android counterpart. The reason? The iOS platform had specific libraries that were not only more challenging to integrate but also had to be carefully chosen to ensure compatibility with other parts of the system. The libraries were an essential part of the upcoming backlog, but they were creating hurdles that slowed our progress.

As the Scrum Master, I decided to set up a parallel tech spike Sprint dedicated entirely to research. I tasked one of our iOS developers with exploring the best libraries for the upcoming backlog items. This parallel Sprint allowed the developer to dive deeper into potential libraries, test them in isolation, and identify the most efficient, scalable options for our project. This way, instead of having the iOS team struggle with integration issues during the main Sprint, they could work ahead and resolve potential blockers, ensuring smoother development in the long run. It was a dedicated space for research and experimentation, and it paid off by allowing us to fine-tune our iOS development strategy without compromising the main Sprint in progress.

The Andon Cord Meeting

This is strictly to remove impediments and blockers. Not a meeting to be underestimated but can be scheduled according to the consensus that the team arrives at. Let your team talk about blockers and analyzing dependencies. While Scrum recommends backlog refinement sessions to do the same, the purpose of having an Andon Cord meeting is to apprise the team of the value of pulling the Andon Cord. Speak up when there is a blocker; don't wait for it to solve.

Working Backward (BDD, RDD, TDD)

Up to 2006 at least, Amazon had a known culture of working backward, like writing a press release document and then understanding of what's possible in the product, what the customer experience should be, what a user manual should look like, what an FAQ document looks like, and so on. By tweaking this one implementation, the team could organize interaction with the client in a way that the product releases are designed backward.

The concept of working backward can be seen as a broader philosophy that aligns with acceptance criteria in development, as well as methodologies like behavior-driven development (BDD), test-driven development (TDD), and even README-driven development. All these approaches focus on understanding the desired end state from the customer's perspective, setting clear expectations, and continuously refining the product's direction during its development.

This philosophy highlights the importance of defining success upfront – whether in the form of acceptance criteria, user manuals, or FAQs – and ensuring that the product meets these expectations throughout the development process. This idea resonates with various agile methods where continuous refinement of the product and its deliverables is a central tenet.

In essence, Amazon's working backward method is an example of building with the end goal in mind, making sure that the customer's needs and the product's success are well-understood before coding begins.

Through Team Structures: Cross-Pollinating Teams

Create temporary cross-departmental teams that bring together diverse expertise, breathing new life into stagnant processes. Picture a marketing team working closely with engineers on a fresh customer experience concept.

I recently worked on a product evaluating LLMs, and we realized there was a disconnect between the sales team and the product we were building. We weren't using language that resonated with the end users. It was the marketing team that stepped in, adopting different user personas, and helped us rethink the customer experience. While we communicated clearly about what was feasible and what wasn't, the collaboration set clear expectations and brought a fresh approach, thanks to the cross-pollination of ideas.

I'm reminded of a similar experience from school. There was a team of nuns who would occasionally step in to teach specific chapters, even if another faculty member was assigned to the class. The lessons they imparted were not just based on textbook knowledge but drawn from their real-life experiences. I remember Sister Lynette, from the Loreto Convent, teaching us mental math, despite our regular math teacher, Ms. Sonia, being present. As a student, I wondered why someone else would teach a section, but in hindsight, the examples Sister Lynette shared were based on real-world scenarios. Her unique perspective added depth and freshness to the subject.

For instance, when teaching mental math, she used examples from her own experience of budgeting for the convent's daily expenses – calculating how much food was needed for the day based on the number of nuns and visitors or how to divide limited resources across various needs. Her approach made the math feel more practical and tangible. It wasn't just about memorizing formulas; it was about applying them in real situations. This unique perspective added depth and freshness to the subject, making it not only more relatable but also far more memorable.

The Saviors

You could have a guild of team leaders who are more experienced than the developers working on a team, and if a project is behind schedule, the guild can step in – not just to take over the project but to mentor and guide the development team through the recovery process. The developers get a break from the pressure of a lagging project while simultaneously having the opportunity to absorb new techniques, tools, and ways of thinking about problem-solving. The developers are given a break from a project that is not up to the schedule, and the retrospective that follows should be outside in – a comparison of how the team leads recovered the project, if at all, and what the developers were doing wrong.

Agile Coaches: To achieve true organizational agility, it's crucial to focus not only on frameworks but also on the nuanced understanding of human behavior. Agile coaches excel at fostering this agility by guiding teams toward the principles of the Agile Manifesto – continuous improvement, transparency, and adaptability. The following narrative illustrates how Agile coaches create an environment where teams flourish, reinforcing the value of "people over process."

1. **Agile Coaches As Observers and Guides**

   Agile coaches act as silent observers, offering valuable insights when teams stray from Agile principles. They notice subtle signs – such as insufficient flexibility or lack of inspection – and provide timely guidance to realign efforts. These coaches are not there to enforce rules but to empower teams to self-correct and grow.

   For example, a Scrum Master I worked with exemplified this approach. Rather than pushing for delivery, he created space for learning and growth. He highlighted mistakes constructively, steering the team in the right direction while fostering a culture of continuous improvement. His approach ensured that every setback became an opportunity to adapt and evolve.

2. **The Importance of Sustained Internal Coaching**

One of my colleagues in the insurance sector shared a story that underscores the value of ongoing coaching. Their company once engaged an external Agile coach who successfully implemented Agile practices. However, after the coach left, the organization gradually reverted to its old waterfall habits. This highlights a critical lesson: Agile transformation requires continuous reinforcement by internal coaches who can embed agility into the organization's DNA.

3. **Facilitative Leadership in Action**

Agile coaches embody facilitative leadership, providing the environment for teams to thrive. Rather than imposing rigid processes, they encourage experimentation and learning. This aligns perfectly with Agile's emphasis on empowering individuals over adhering strictly to processes. In this context, Agile coaches guide teams to explore innovative solutions while maintaining focus on delivering value to the customer.

4. **The Human Element: A Lesson in People Over Process**

I want to mention a fond memory from my time teaching at an NGO in Chandigarh (Theatre Age). During a class, I asked a bright student to remove his birthday cap, which he wore proudly. His confidence visibly diminished, and he struggled to answer questions. Realizing my mistake, I returned the cap, and his confidence – and accuracy –

returned instantly. This simple act reinforced the importance of understanding and addressing human needs to unlock potential. In Agile terms, this is the essence of psychological safety, where people perform best when they feel supported and respected. By prioritizing the child's emotional need (the cap) over strict classroom rules, the scenario exemplified "people over process."

5. **A Culture of Continuous Learning and Improvement**

    The role of Agile coaches extends beyond guiding teams – they foster a culture of curiosity and continuous improvement. They are the champions of organizational agility, ensuring that teams remain adaptable, resilient, and customer-focused. They also help identify wasteful practices and realign efforts toward delivering genuine value.

Agile coaches play a pivotal role in achieving organizational agility by blending technical expertise with deep empathy and understanding of human behavior. By fostering an environment of psychological safety, continuous learning, and empowerment, they help teams navigate the complexities of Agile transformation. This is not merely about adhering to Agile frameworks but about embedding a mindset that prioritizes adaptability, collaboration, and, most importantly, people.

Retrospective Templates

There are plenty of ways to innovate the retrospective. While we have a detailed section in this chapter on retros, let's just give you a simple idea of how you could help your team grow. All innovations on retrospectives should make your teams more honest. So, helping them admit where they went wrong individually is a crucial part to this innovation. For instance, instead of the regular template of "What went well," "What didn't go well," and "Action items," try "What I could have done better" and "What worked for the product." This one analysis should make your participants learn and grow for the better. If you recall, this connects directly with the journaling we suggested in the first chapter. More on this when we explore retrospectives in detail.

Why, What, and How

Suppose each team member silently reflects on three questions:

a. **Why**: What is the purpose of my work today? What value will it bring?

b. **What**: What are my key tasks and priorities for today?

c. **How**: What obstacles might I face? How will I overcome them?

This format, like other innovations and facilitation techniques, depends on how your team responds to daily planning. If it helps sort their minds before work, nothing like it, else you can always keep such practices optional.

Whenever I donned the role of a Scrum Master, I simply could not restrict my meetings to the context of the project. I would love analogies, making people think of the purpose of their work, even redefining their role in the company. So often would I find the right people doing the wrong thing.

Mad Hatter Standups for Cultural Issues

Try having a lesser priority standup (not a DSM), in a more casual environment, maybe a team lunch. Don't record statuses; don't record anything at all. Say, everyone writes their cultural issues on cards, shuffles them, and draws another's card to present and offer solutions. This will foster team bonding over issues they might not discuss while working.

Feature-Based Teams and XP

Feature-based teams are cross-functional groups responsible for delivering complete user-centric features in an agile environment. They possess all the necessary skills (development, design, testing, etc.) to bring a feature from conception to completion, fostering end-to-end ownership and accountability for the selected feature. In contrast, many teams have a traditional approach of component-based teams, where different components of engineering get together and work on a project. Imagine a project which involves redesigning a music streaming app with feature-based teams. How would you structure this project team? One possible implementation is given below:

Team Size: Three Feature Teams (eight to ten people each) and working on the following features.

- **Feature Team 1: Personalized Recommendations**: This team focuses on improving the recommendation engine, leveraging user data, listening habits, and AI to personalize playlists and suggestions.

- **Feature Team 2: Enhanced Social Features**: This team develops features like collaborative playlists, shared listening experiences, and artist communities to foster social interaction within the app.

- **Feature Team 3: Podcast Integration**: This team integrates podcasts into the app seamlessly, offering discovery, playback, and organization features for podcast listeners.

Ericsson, a leading telecommunications company, implemented a case study comparing two different team structures for software development: feature teams and component teams. This study, conducted by Craig Larman and Bas Vodde, documented their findings in the book *Scaling Lean & Agile Development*. It was concluded that while both structures have their merits, Ericsson's case study suggests feature teams generally lead to faster delivery, higher quality, and greater customer satisfaction, with increased team morale as a bonus. Feature-based teams are gathering attention and execution everywhere. In our innovation, we could add the flavor of XP practices with feature-based teams, especially pair programming. I've seen firsthand when two people solve one problem, the culture of cross-functionality and collaboration, and even greater depth of the product in question comes to the surface.

Innovation Through Lean UX

This innovation is based on practices discussed in the book *Lean UX* and our experiences based on processes where design isn't lean during implementation.

Before we dig deeper, however, we need to understand why some design practices aren't lean at all. If a prototyping method were to be called lean, it would, in the bare minimum, eliminate waste. If your designers are working on exercises that are never used, or designing without review, or actual feedback, their effort is not lean anymore. I've heard people in the automotive industry proudly saying that lean is something that they know very well. But you'll have plenty of cases that engineers' designs are not reviewed properly for lack of resources. How is that lean then? Keep the principles of Lean in mind, and keep questioning yourself. Is this activity following lean?

Structuring Teams for Lean Design

Ideally, a lean design team would involve marketeers, engineers, quality assurance people, and all sorts of cross-functionalities. For your prototype to cater to all segments of the product development life cycle. Consider a simple meditation mobile app. A marketeer would probably bring in points of view of target audiences and personas, based on real-time information. A quality engineer would tell you about things that design shouldn't have – maybe like a single point of failure. Developers would give you a brief complexity and feasibility analysis – whether you're making a design decision that is ultimately convertible to the development stage or not.

Meeting Themes Around Lean UX

Keeping meetings around topics that would steer the team's attention to Lean UX is one way of building lean teams and innovating agile further. Here, we try to **minimize handoffs** and focus on building cross-functional teams, while at the same time solve a problem and address a feature. For instance, at the end of every Sprint or a major feature delivered or even at a point where your team finds fit, **discuss the problem being solved**. This might sound like the "Product over Project" meeting, but it's not. Here, you're moving outward in. It can mean something as simple as taking an element in a product and grilling it down, as we explain in the next subsection.

Calls to Action Evaluation Meeting: An Example of Minimizing Waste in Design

Somewhere in a big project, you'd forget the flow of all calls to action. You'd like to visit them, again, wouldn't you? Such a meeting could ask critical questions such as "Is the CTA easy to see and recognize? Is the CTA's value proposition and intent clear? Does it use appropriate colors, contrast, and size? Is the CTA located where users expect it to be? What do the analytics tell us about its performance?" When the meeting starts, you could create a list of all CTAs across main user journey touchpoints on the website. Note their location, label, design, and intended action. If the product is live, gather available analytics on CTA click-through rates, conversion rates, and any relevant heatmap data. Involve different kinds of users for this meeting – UX designers/researchers, content strategists, developers (if potential changes are technically complex), marketing, and stakeholders (if relevant). Such meetings can make you see your designs through specific lenses which can be easily avoided otherwise. Understanding what is relevant, and what isn't becomes far easier then.

Notice that it's not just about Product over Project; it's also about not creating waste in any part of the product. There might be many ways to let everyone design. For instance, make sure everyone gets a hand at sketching a solution. Ask everyone in the team to make a sketch on paper for a particular feature. Introduce them to design thinking, wireframing, points of failure, and validation – make it collaborative. Let these sketches be submitted to designers for more thought and translation. It can help in better ideation and can also include feedback and collaboration. If you sincerely follow the principle of Lean UX and are colocated with your team, you'll find that such practices once a while help people think which in turn leads to design that doesn't have to let users think.

Lean UX is a big topic, and I'd encourage you to go through material dedicated entirely for this subject, because it shapes your mind on a different pathway.

As an author, I intended to set the stage for a user to tweak through well-established schools of thought and create meetings or boards around their concepts. It's more than obvious that not one style would fit all and not all styles would fit into one cycle. It's also obvious that so many different kinds of meetings will not fit into the same project. Pick, choose, inspect, adapt, and repeat. Happy agility!

How Companies Are Pushing the Boundaries of Agile

Let's look at three simple examples of quantifying agility and measuring the impact of creative agile practices in leading organizations. These examples give you an idea of game-changing innovation that is happening in organizations that could inspire your next idea.

Case Study: Spotify's Symphony of Squads, Tribes, Chapters, and Guilds

Spotify's unique structure replaced rigid hierarchies with empowered, self-organizing teams. Their "Squads" (average seven to nine people) focus on individual features, delivering value quickly. "Tribes" (around 40-150 people) group related squads tackling a common product area. "Chapters" (10-30 members) foster expertise in specific areas like testing or security. "Guilds" connect individuals across tribes for knowledge sharing. This intricate setup boasts impressive results:

> **Reduced Lead Time by 50%:** Faster development cycles translate to faster product launches and market responsiveness. (Source: https://engineering.atspotify.com/)

> **Increased Employee Satisfaction by 20%:** Empowered teams with ownership and autonomy lead to happier and more engaged employees. (Source: https://www.lifeatspotify.com/)

> **Improved Product Quality and Innovation:** Diverse perspectives and knowledge sharing within tribes and guilds drive creative solutions. (Source: https://engineering.atspotify.com/2014/03/spotify-engineering-culture-part-1/)

While complex to implement, Spotify's approach demonstrates the power of tailoring agile practices to specific needs. Note that the saviors concept we mentioned in the previous section was borrowed from the guild implementation in Spotify but in a different manner.

Case Study: Haier's Microenterprise Revolution

Haier's radical approach replaced traditional management with self-managed "microenterprises" (MEs). Each ME (50–200 employees) acts like a mini company with its own CEO, CFO, and marketing manager. MEs autonomously make decisions, manage resources, and compete. This experiment has yielded remarkable outcomes:

- **Doubled Revenue in Five Years**: Empowered teams react quicker to market changes, leading to faster growth. (Source: https://www.haier.com/global/)

- **Increased Employee Engagement**: Ownership and accountability drive higher motivation and performance. (Source: https://www.haier.com/global/)

- **Enhanced Innovation**: Freed from bureaucracy, teams experiment and develop innovative solutions. (Source: https://www.haier.com/global/)

Case Study: Netflix's Chaos Monkey – Embracing Controlled Mayhem

Netflix's engineering team intentionally injects random failures into their systems using the "Chaos Monkey" tool. This simulates real-world disruptions, helping them identify and fix vulnerabilities before they impact customers. This proactive approach has yielded quantifiable benefits:

- **Reduced Downtime by 90%:** Proactive troubleshooting prevents major outages, ensuring service reliability. (Source: `https://netflixtechblog.com/tagged/chaos-monkey`)

- **Increased Engineering Team Confidence:** Knowing they can handle failures fosters a culture of resilience and innovation. (Source: `https://netflixtechblog.com/tagged/chaos-monkey`)

- **Improved System Architecture:** Identifying and fixing weak points leads to more robust and resilient systems. (Source: `https://netflixtechblog.com/tagged/chaos-monkey`)

Netflix's experiment showcases how embracing controlled chaos can be a powerful tool for building resilient and adaptable systems within an agile environment.

These three case studies give you an example of how companies are tweaking umbrellas like agile and introducing practices that can fit well underneath the main cover. It does pay off, if your product engineering teams have thinking leaders who strategize organizational structures, transformation, and coach them to higher scale. As we describe later, in all of it, there can be self-checks of keeping agile to its true north.

Keeping Agile to Its True North

Dr. Jeff Sutherland and JJ Sutherland have put it brilliantly in their article, "Debunking Sustainable Pace with Dr. Jeff Sutherland and JJ Sutherland," and we reiterate the thought for you here. This is an article about the Agile Manifesto and the concept of sustainable pace. It discusses the original intent of sustainable pace, which was to allow teams to maintain high performance without burning out. The article argues that sustainable pace has been misinterpreted and misused as an excuse for mediocrity. Similarly, it mentions that agile was often taken to be a canvas of doing what you want, which it was not. Like we mentioned in our first chapter, we mentioned that we can tweak agile methods, but not its values. The principles remain the same.

Summary

This chapter took us through a basic way of understanding execution within principles, but not limiting ourselves to Scrum ceremonies or frameworks already laid down for us. It dares us to think on our own, keeping our values intact. The next chapter takes you through why such practices might be more relevant now than ever before.

Further Reading

Lean UX: Creating Great Products with Agile Teams, Third Edition - by Jeff Gothelf (Author), Josh Seiden (Author)

The Lean Mindset – by Mary Poppendieck (Author), Tom Poppendieck (Author)

Exercise

Redesign your room by identifying things that you no longer need. Would you get rid of them or reposition them? Why haven't you used them for a long time? Train your mind to think of yourself as a user for your room, and customize your experience, with a conscious mindset.

CHAPTER 4

Voices from the Field

We take a pause in our agile playground activities and show you what people are saying in agile. This would show you how some of the previously mentioned innovations are important and how organizational agility and being agile as a society and as people helps for lesser stress at work. This chapter provides an interview and a few surveys to better understand how agile is being implemented, the kind of challenges that people face because of lack of agility, and what our comments are on the same. Such situations can bring in a lot of situational awareness, which in turn encourages the need for healthy cultures and quick response.

Interview: Lack of Agility in Education

Here, we interviewed a leading expert in the field of nuclear medicine in India, who gave us insight into how research is held. For the sake of anonymity, we do not disclose the name and university here, but these details are accurate as of 2024 and are in fact a standing challenge to education implementation. The details given would tell the reader that it's not possible to fabricate such information, and the narrative shows real pain points that professors are facing in higher education – nuclear medicine being our chosen case study.

[Question]: Hello doctor. Thanks for the interview. Let's start by coming straight to the point. Could you give us a broad idea of how nuclear medicine education suffers in India? Any 3 challenges from the top of your mind?

© Kanika Sud 2025
K. Sud, *Customizable Agile Development*, https://doi.org/10.1007/979-8-8688-1055-8_4

[Answer]: Hello. The credit system of the curriculum is a real challenge, which I can elaborate for you later in this interview. Training gets hindered because of the way hospitals are equipped. Most importantly, when students are admitted, they are unskilled, and eligibility criteria are vaguely defined. Even though attempts are ongoing to improve this, the eligibility guidelines already defined are skipped during the actual admission process, because to fill in seats, people from many backgrounds are admitted, which again isn't the recommended way of doing so.

[Question]: Thanks. So, if we talk of the credit system now. What is it, and how is it a challenge?

[Answer]: A credit is basically a quantified version of a teaching learning hour, that is a goal for a teacher to be able to achieve optimum progress. The process becomes complicated because of the way credits are spanned out. Say, a credit is 15 teaching learning hours. A teacher needs a minimum of three credits, and five credits are good. Hence, we can say, 45-75 hours, per subject in one semester is what teachers are aiming at. Here, the system becomes more complex, when teachers must teach five subjects, because of lack of resources, and because of **an organizational decision, which comes top down**. This means we are looking at 225 to 375 hours per semester. This comes down to 29 hours per week, against the standard recommendation of 16 hours per week. Effectively, a teacher takes five teaching hours per day. On the face of it, that sounds nothing but combined with administrative tasks - meetings, minutes of the meetings, lab docs, attendance management piles up, coordination tasks, audit documents, pedagogy methods being logged, tools introduced - all of this kills the soul and hampers thinking. You're doing 5 hours of teaching, and on an average 4 hours of administrative hours. It is to be noted that these administrative practices are good, but these documents do not belong to the ones who deliver the curriculum. Website content authoring is also given to us, for technical writing and proofreading. There need to be separate teams for such tasks. We could have done so much better if we this process had more resources to manage the administrative tasks, and **optimum workload.**.

[Question]: What's the mindset clash here? Is there nobody to understand that the faculty is facing such a problem?

[Answer]: The organization currently thinks that it is a problem of a student-to-teacher ratio. From 15 students under one teacher, the organization brought it down to 10:1. The problem, however, is a more human workload problem. Of what capacity the teacher must deliver, and whether he has a say in it or not. Changes are being proposed, however. It is yet to be seen, how they play out. The main problem again will be that the right questions may not be asked. That nobody might ask us whether we feel productive enough. Nobody might solve it in a manner that encourages productivity, but it might be seen as a KPI driven problem. What we need is a **frank collaboration** between all parties.

[Question]: Let's talk of student admission processes. You've briefly mentioned the problem. Again, given that people are admitted from unwanted backgrounds, do you think the process lacks inspection and adaptation? A lack of honesty to self maybe?

[Answer]: This is a problem that leads to every other. Student admission is connected to revenue generation. This is a falsified concept, and unethical too. For any professional course, you cannot let people in, who do not pass eligibility standards, and commercializing such education by compromising standards is not the right way out. As far as the keywords inspection and adaptation are concerned, this certainly requires a lot of inspection, from policy makers itself. The operational budget currently comes only from the revenue we generate, and no alternate source of funding is clearly placed in the picture. Global universities have set an example by decoupling funding for research and training. Look at Stanford, HZDR – Helmholtz-Zentrum Dresden-Rossendorf - these are dedicated research institutes, and their funding is managed apart from teaching activities. Combing the budget of the two is the fundamental flaw that we need to look at, in India.

[Question]: Training within hospitals. This was the third challenge you pointed out. What do you have to say about this?

[Answer]: Training is a constant challenge, because of lack of infrastructure and time. The same teacher who is keeping pace with credits and administrative tasks, is now put in the role of a trainer. It is more of a problem with the trainee, because of the quality of the training imparted - it will not be ideal, and the purpose of it all is defeated. The root of such problems comes from inefficient finance management. Budgets are not delivery friendly. It's that simple. Funding, funding, funding. That can solve the first step for many such problems. But it's not the funds really. It's about convincing the senior management about the need for such funds. Unless it's a full-blown problem, such areas will never be anticipated or foreseeable and will not be handled.

[Question]: If we give you a hypothetical situation, where you get to make the policy of your department and manage funding as well, do you think that the following points would solve your problem to some extent? Comment.

1. **Delivery of curriculum over comprehensive documentation**, or at least separation of concerns in a way, that the workload of the docs is balanced between who documents and who delivers.
   Eliminating waste in general by not attaching value to tasks, which do not have worth.

2. **Frank collaboration, inspection, adaptation** and will to resolve impediments quickly.

3. **Limit the work in hand**, and not make employees deliver over their optimum capacity.

4. **Creating a pull system**, where a teacher decides how much he can deliver and when, rather than a push system, where teachers are told of KPIs, without taking into consideration of what they can deliver.

5. **Reorienting the focus of the organization towards the effort of teachers**, rather than physical deliverables like docs or administrative tasks, which teachers were not made for.

[Answer]: Yes, it would solve a great deal, especially by the second point. I mean if someone's listening and adapting, it's a matter of principle and value - and that can mean a social change for the better.

Recap

This interview reveals systemic challenges in nuclear medicine education, beyond just individual teaching difficulties. The professor's experience suggests a need for better resource allocation, workload management, and a more responsive approach to feedback. While broader societal factors can play a role, addressing immediate issues within the system itself is crucial for improvement. In essence, the lack of agility in this system stems from its inflexibility, bureaucratic nature, top-down approach, financial limitations, and misplaced priorities. These factors make it difficult to adapt to changing needs, implement new ideas, and respond efficiently to challenges, hindering the overall progress and effectiveness of nuclear medicine education. Now, here comes the scale – I've spoken to professors in digital marketing, disaster management, sustainability, architecture, and so many different fields. They are of the view that education systems are stifling their own running engine, by not letting flexibility set in. By not accepting feedback. By not being lean in some cases. You'll have teachers who tell you of their workload that they cannot even teach properly because of the number of classes they take. You'll have teachers who speak of attempts to make all teachers climb a tree, when what you have in store is that every teacher is cut out for a different skill set. This and many other problems crowd the teaching space, at least in India. It's time to factor in agile models, which we'll discuss at the end of the lesson.

Before we walk off to the next section, we would want you to look at the following stats to give you a picture of what this situation is at a global level, and not just in India:

Teacher Shortages:

Source: UNESCO Institute for Statistics (UIS)

Data: As of 2020, there was a global shortage of 9 million teachers, expected to rise to 13 million by 2030.

Impact: Larger class sizes reduced individual attention and potential lack of access to education for certain groups.

Teacher Workload:

Source: Education International (EI)

Data: A 2020 survey found that 71% of teachers reported feeling stressed or burned out on a daily basis.

Impact: Decreased teacher well-being, potential for lower quality instruction, and increased risk of turnover.

Teacher Salaries:

Source: OECD Education at a Glance 2023

Data: On average, teacher salaries are 11% lower than those of similarly qualified workers in other professions.

Impact: Difficulty attracting and retaining talented teachers, especially in high-cost areas.

Student Learning Outcomes:

Source: PISA 2018 Results (OECD)

Data: There is a significant correlation between teacher–student ratio and student achievement scores in many countries.

Impact: Lower student learning outcomes and potential for widening achievement gaps.

The education sector, of course, doesn't revolve around only the lack of agility. It revolves around a great deal of other factors.

Agility would involve discussions and resolutions and then moving forward. Problems being documented and not being addressed honestly is the antithesis of agility. What education is facing now is the predecessor of the society we are teaching and mentoring and hence the need to introduce agility at its very core. Now on to the surveys.

Conducting Surveys

For the rest of this chapter, we'll substantiate a point we make with the surveys we took, showing you responses and charts. Let's start with giving you an idea of how many people have adopted agile so far, from a set of 50 working professionals (Figure 4-1). The survey had no geographical restriction. It was collected by rotating a form in executive groups who came from world over.

Survey Results: Agile Adaptation And Associated Challenges

This data is derived from 50 responses

Has your organization fully, partially or not adopted scrum at all?

Did you have a clear scrum implementation plan when starting your scrum journey?

If you answered "No", what challenges did you face in the absence of a clear Scrum implementation plan?

Partially 61.5%

Fully 38.5%

Yes 46.2%

Maybe 23.1%

No 30.8%

Resistance to change 30%

Difficulty in defining roles 20%

No direction 10%

Unclear objective 40%

Have you been part of non agile methodologies? If so, which one?

What according to you would make a perfect scrum irrespective of the hurdles?

Waterfall (66.7%)

Spiral Model (0%)

V-Model (0%)

Saw Tooth Model (0%)

Unified Process Model (0%)

Only followed in my company (22.2%)

Currently working in an envt. (11.1%)

Estimating work accurately (53.8%)

Team collaboration (69.2%)

Balancing documentation (23.1%)

Management support (23.1%)

Clear task visibility (7.7%)

Figure 4-1. *Survey Results for Agile Adaptation and Associated Challenges in a Group of 50 Professionals*

If you notice, for anyone who truly appreciates the value of agility, they'd tell you that for 61.5% leaders showing partially agile is not that great a response. What is also concerning is the response of some of the employees as "I'm currently working in an environment which doesn't follow agile, and they are struggling to get things done. Developers are resolving things without proper knowledge of bugs, and QA teams test with the same knowledge," when we asked them about which agile methods do they follow and to comment subjectively if necessary.

Since "team collaboration" is given enough weightage by people who implement Scrum and I can tell you firsthand that it's a team's willingness to appreciate agility and a leader's vision to mold them so, that works in the favor of the product. Choose whatever framework you will; those principles that fail or succeed are through the team's synergy. It is primarily because of this reason that we discussed facilitation techniques in the previous chapter as an important way of innovation. Facilitation cannot be ignored in a world where team collaboration is a must.

Real-World Insights from Various Sectors

Next, we spoke to people from various sectors, ranging from design, automotive, financial services, software industry, and so on.

Design forms a very important part of engineering. How it's implemented and estimated often determines the smoothness of the rest of the engineering process. And yet, people who work on the field know that it's always easier to preach – the real situation is far from perfect.

A senior product designer, who preferred remaining anonymous, flatly told us that even after having worked with teams across the globe, not many were adaptive in the design process. Here's what our designer friend had to say: "Many companies take design lightly or in the constraints of the service contract involved. We are never given a chance to interview a real customer or create personas as we would like to. In many projects, developers are not brought into the picture until much later because of resource costs involved. In one project, I remember making animations in Figma, and then later, much later, when developers started working on the animations, they told me they wanted Lottie files made in Adobe After Effects. Their case could not have been implemented by Figma animations at all. The entire design cycle had to be revisited, because the contract did not allow for regular design reviews by developers. Then of course comes the process of design itself. Designs were passed from one designer to the other, because of workload. There was no pull system. Everyone worked 2x their productivity. It wasn't lean in that sense. Sometimes the client enforced a timeline which wasn't conducive to ideation and concepts we've learnt. The industry is far apart from what we study, and maybe it's governed by financial constraints rather than an actual love for design. Good designs are made for projecting case studies to future leads, not for understanding nuances of the product itself."

We spoke with a senior product owner in the financial services sector. It was great to understand how an agile coach was hired from BCG and Accenture in their firm for agile transformation. There were, however, minor problems still being noticed in the implementation. Change management was not handled, since Scrum and Kanban did not officially lay down ways of handling scope creep. People around the world interpreted agile and scrum the way they wanted to, without seeking balance between some traditional methods and using agile methods for transparency and adaptation between short turnaround time cycles. For the case in question, the senior product owner we spoke with said that a business analyst to document the project execution the traditional way, in addition to the PO's management documents of user stories and epics, would help them achieve balance. Also, digging further, we found out that the agile coach had left their functional area after he found that the team was a self-sustaining agile team (I mentioned a similar case in one of my previous chapters; seems agile coaches when hired externally are assumed to introduce agile, not inspire agility. There is a difference, and we miss that difference). Perhaps a better approach would be an agile audit of sorts, by agile coaches, to see if teams are facing challenges in its adoption. In this company, the production release cycles were as long as years, and so, by nature of contracts and habit, managers tend to adopt "Scrum" as a process, not as a framework. They work under the name of Scrum, but in effect, they implement waterfall.

We asked people about the kind of challenges they face in Scrum and agile methods at large. Again, the survey results shown in Figure 4-2 are from a dataset of the same 50 people who responded to the first set of questions.

Resistance to change (53.8%)

Lack of management support (53.8%)

Lack of understanding of scrum (53.8%)

Inadequate training and education (23.1%)

Poorly defined product backlog (76.9%)

Inefficient sprint planning (61.5%)

Challenges in estimating work (38.5%)

Poor team collaboration (46.2%)

Insufficient transparency (46.2%)

Overemphasis on documentation (15.4%)

Figure 4-2. *Survey Results for the Kind of Challenges People Face in Scrum*

If you notice, not many people face any documentation challenges in Scrum. In fact, Scrum and agile does not pressurize anyone for documentation at all – it says that deliverables are more important than comprehensive documentation. We had purposefully added that option to see how many people still choose it to understand where people stand at the kind of documentation being inserted. What interests me as an agile practitioner are the first seven options. I'll address these problems and their solutions in the next chapter when we investigate how we can go about creating custom frameworks in agile, suiting our organizational needs. Till then, it's worthwhile to keep an eye out on these challenges and identify your own, so that while transforming your organization into an agile ready organization, you work on a problem-solution-design basis, where the solution comes from the core of the problem itself.

Before concluding this chapter, I decided to speak with my own school teacher, Mrs. Reetu Sharma, an educator with 33 years of experience at the Convent of Loreto, about how values matter in every workplace, including teaching. Here's what she shared:

> *"Introspection is one of the most important values in teaching. Teaching cannot exist without introspection. Each set of students is different, and how they learn is different. We can only build better citizens if we continuously improve ourselves. Continuous improvement is part of human behavior and applies to every profession. How can teaching be an exception? For instance, through constant introspection, we adapt our teaching methods to match the dynamics of the information age. If I simply read from a book, children may not engage with me as they did 20 years ago. Methods have changed, the environment has changed—and so must we.*
>
> *Shorter milestones, like those you mentioned in the Agile Manifesto, help students by allowing them to be assessed on smaller goals. It gives them a sense of achievement. For example, we transitioned from a half-yearly examination system to a semester system, which assesses students on smaller objectives. This helps them identify their problems earlier and provides a chance to learn in better ways, avoiding repeated mistakes.*
>
> *Policies may change over time, but students are more important to us than any process or tool. Exercising common sense for the best interests of education, even if it means going against policy, is essential—even if it risks failure.*
>
> *Talk sessions, for instance, bring out the best in children. Have you ever wondered why? It's the ability to express. A face-to-face conversation adds visuals, body language, context, and so many elements a teacher can utilize to shape a child's understanding.*

Commitment, focus, openness, respect, and courage are not just values for corporate frameworks or workplace cultures. These are universal values. Period. Absorbing these values and using common sense alongside them is essential. Every profession, including teaching, draws on these same core principles."

Summary

We examined the importance of agility in education and other sectors through interviews and surveys, highlighting systemic challenges such as workload imbalance, rigid structures, and inadequate resource allocation. Excessive administrative tasks, poorly defined eligibility criteria, insufficient training infrastructure–burdened educators, how agile methods are often misapplied, frameworks frequently reverting to traditional waterfall models due to organizational inertia, and the value of introspection, adaptability, and prioritizing people over rigid policies in all professions starting from teaching children – all this goes to show the importance of underscoring the broader need for agility to foster continuous improvement and better outcomes across sectors. Reaching out to industry experts is very helpful and is always an enjoyable exercise indeed. See you in the next lesson!

CHAPTER 5

Customized Frameworks

Up to here, what we've understood is how human tendencies affect agility and the lack thereof. We also tapped into some of them to understand how facilitation can change the game. We investigated some real-time interviews by people who've been affected by circumstances that do not provide room for agility. We investigated good and bad implementations and saw how honesty and transparency were at the root of whatever framework you're following.

Keeping all of this as a post to hang on to, let's now look at what a framework in agile means. Note that this chapter does not help you to make a framework just yet but helps inspect what goes into a framework. This chapter also forms the crux of the book, because it centers around our main theme of customizable Agile. We've taken the help of scenarios from the industry (my own experiences), which show how tweaking agile without adhering to its principles can lead to fatigue, toxicity, loss of good workforce, increase in cost, lack of quality, and more unforeseen disasters.

What Makes a Framework?

We'll start by looking into what makes a framework: actors and team structures, artifacts, and events. We'll also see why leading frameworks like Scrum speak of values. We will introduce emotional concepts of team culture so that while building a framework, we do not forget people.

© Kanika Sud 2025
K. Sud, *Customizable Agile Development*, https://doi.org/10.1007/979-8-8688-1055-8_5

Actors and Team Structures

You need people to work in any setting, agile or not. And these people are our actors when you refer to frameworks. They work in accountability matrices, toward goals or under a common umbrella with or without defined roles – but toward common goals. Undermining team topologies is a huge mistake. You'll get so absorbed in daily work that you won't know where you're going wrong, whereas the real issue could be that the actors and their accountabilities in your framework could be either too complex or too loosely defined for your own good. When you study actors and team structures together, you realize that any such study would be incomplete without understanding complex adaptive systems (CAS). Which is why we take them up next, before we inspect actors and teams deeply. What are complex adaptive systems anyway? Let's find out.

Complex Adaptive Systems and Their Importance

An organization, in effect, is a complex adaptive system. It fits the definition perfectly because it is a network of interconnected components and is constantly adaptive. Moreover, the behaviour of an organization is always emergent – meaning, that it cannot be predicted by the behaviour of its individual components. It's the synergy that plays a part. Any interaction can serve as an input for the system itself directly or indirectly. When playing a part of these systems, components behave locally and may or may not be aware of the entire system.

> *Organizations should be viewed as complex and adaptive mechanisms rather than mechanistic and linear systems.*
>
> —Naomi

Complex adaptive systems are extremely interesting and wider than the scope of the book, but the reader is advised to keep studying this awesome topic and simultaneously observe and adapt changing behaviour of peers and team members.

Understanding Team Topologies

The second topic we mentioned above was team structures. Team structures can be influenced by team sizing, team skill set, communication pathways, component- or feature-based teams, and much more. The main keyword remains synergy. When you speak of synergy, one wonders how best to place teams. Anyone who's been working with teams knows how bad team structures can affect everything – from product health and cost overruns to mind wellness. Let's start with team sizing.

Team Sizing

Before we go further, recall the team sizes that you have worked with, and question yourself if team sizes have affected the nature of your work – if so how. Write it down somewhere, so that you can visit it at the end of this section.

Team size naturally affects the complexity of the team's work. It is not just because of the interactions and communication pathways, though these two are the most visible consequences of team size – but what plays a subtle role in teams is trust. According to anthropologist Robin Dunbar, we can maintain close relationships with

- Around five individuals or hold them in our working memory

- Deeply trust up to 15 people

- Trust mutually up to 50 individuals

- Remember around 150 people's capabilities

Come to think of it, how many people did you hang out with when in school? What would be the group size? You weren't consciously forming a team, but those were the people you trusted the most. It should not be a surprise if the same trait is carried over to the workplace.

This insightful data has influenced the structure of Scrum Teams. Here's what the Scrum Guide says:

> *The Scrum Team is small enough to remain nimble and large enough to complete significant work within a Sprint, typically 10 or fewer people. In general, we have found that smaller teams communicate better and are more productive.*
>
> —Scrum Guide

Over a period of time, Scrum practitioners recommended keeping teams between seven and nine members to optimize efficiency. Anything larger and it's advised to split into a Scrum of Scrums, or tribes, or groups, and the like.

Some high-trust organizations divide their teams like so:

5, 15, 50, 150,

where 15 people are divided into teams of five each and so on. But five to eight or seven to nine would not be crossed. I have been part of bigger team sizes where management complexity, difficulty of collaboration, underutilization of talent, problems related with handoffs, lack of focus, and undervaluing empiricism are natural consequences of not dividing bigger teams into microteams.

We would finally say that through experience, good leaders understand optimal team sizes for a project. Your work should never lack resources and time at the cost of a team size. Small team size does not imply a lack of required skill set or burning resources to reduce cost. You cannot force people to work beyond their capacity all the time. A sad reality is that in small companies, so-called "Founders" exact work of nine months in a single month, for revenue and maintaining cash flow. Now, while that changes the synergy overwhelmingly, team sizing is not the problem here. It is the lack of intent on the part of the senior management.

Research into how people interact can be very useful when making our framework within custom agile frameworks. The reader is encouraged to observe his surroundings constantly, to find out how people interact according to team size and various environment triggers. We'll revisit this in the last chapter when we take agility at a cellular level. For now, look at the notes about team sizing you made earlier in this section. Does our rationale relate with any of your experiences? Dig further into the topic of team sizes and human interaction. Happy exploring!

Now, we seek to keep your own observations informed by substantiating any claims on team sizing and complex adaptive systems, with a few scenarios. Let's get straight to them.

Scenario 1: ABCXYZ Corp

Let us look at a scenario where even though Scrum is followed in name, the number of team members and actors become too complex to handle and the result is an extremely sad energy. The reason I used the word sad is that I was part of such a unit. With this scenario, we also get to see how important actors are and how we can apply lean thinking when we make a framework and choose its artifacts.

Imagine a fictitious company called ABCXYZ Corp. Here is how the organization executes Scrum:

1. They combine the Product Owner and the Scrum Master into one.

2. The Scrum Master is silently expected to be an engineering manager.

3. The organization follows a component-based team structure. The software delivery team leads are component leads, so there will be a component for Android, and one Android lead would lead all

Android projects, and any Android developer could reach out to him about how to fix a problem in his ongoing project. Similarly, the design team has their lead, and roughly 30 designers would be led by, say, 2 design leads, and their pain points and progress are taken up in daily meetings with the design lead. Figure 5-1 shows how an Android team looked like.

Figure 5-1. *Component-Based Team Structure*

When this is seen from the perspective of a project,
it becomes something like Figure 5-2.

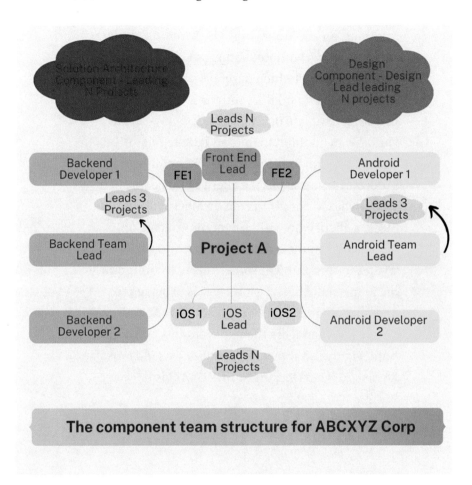

Figure 5-2. *The Component Team Structure from a Project*
Perspective

Keep these visuals in mind, and be ready to refer to
them later, when we inspect the problems with this
structure.

4. Let's put in a communication blast. A manager is expected to talk on multiple channels with the client and the team. There is a weekly status mail to clients, an additional mid-week internal project status meeting, without demos but based on verbal communication (which happens on Microsoft Teams Meet), mandatory minutes of the meeting in a strict template on tools like Confluence and Outlook. In addition to this, add the regular JIRA documentation for user stories. Communication is decentralized as per the client's choice – a client who wishes to communicate on Slack will continue Slack, a client who wishes to communicate on Figma will communicate on Figma, and a client who wishes to communicate on Teams will communicate on Teams. Effectively, a manager is expected to check all places where the client talks and to report back while managing the requirements and delivery both. Figure 5-3 shows how your day would look like if you had been working at ABCXYZ Corp.

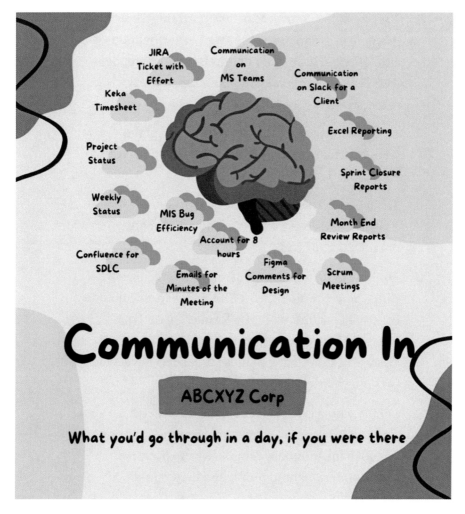

Figure 5-3. *Demonstrating the Communication Blast in ABCXYZ*

5. The pressure for reporting is such that the focus on
    the deliverable is lesser than the focus on "telling"
    the client or the reporting manager that the work
    is done.

6. A group of five Scrum Masters is currently reporting to a delivery manager, no Sprint Review happens, and there are little to no demos internally, neither with the senior management nor the delivery manager.

7. There is no vision of the founder, or any of the team members to scale agile, or speak up regarding solution-oriented management.

8. The icing on the cake, there are very few retrospectives at a team level and none at an organizational level.

9. For timesheet management, efforts were logged thrice: once for the PM on JIRA. Once for the quality control department on MIS forms, to detail out efforts on bugs. And once on Keka (an HR tool). If you won't submit any of these timesheets, you won't get your salaries.

10. People who were real leaders did not receive promotion. People who were one-minute managers or spoke the founders' language were promoted. The founders wanted profit, and they wanted it badly.

Such companies exist in numbers more than we can imagine. I have been a startup founder and failed too, and criticizing another is not my place. Suggestive leadership, however, is something that I look up to, and that stems from problem identification, so we identify the problems that can be identified and solutions that can be suggested must be shared.

Problem Identification in Scenario 1

One would think how we should evaluate this scenario against what should be. The best way to identify problems would be to ask fair questions. Let's see how.

Questioning the Scenario: Cross-Checking with Lean Thinking

Lean thinking, as we explained earlier, helps to minimize waste. The above scenario would not fail if we minimize waste. Well, some of the questions to ask are as follows:

- Are the communication channels leading to waste?

- What is being communicated in all meetings? Is that leading to wasteful thinking or are these meetings productive enough? What kind of time goes into meetings and calls? (Trust me, an extremely capable team lead I knew could not gather the waste time on calls and fruitless activities. His team eventually resigned, because of this one flaw from the senior management).

- How can the client communication process be standardized without compromising client satisfaction?

- When developers and managers look back, can they happily point out the value the project added to their journey? And can they point out the value that they added to the project?

- Are the decisions made with sufficient information? Is there a decision log?

- Is the team empowered and motivated?

- Is the business value of the product road map being assessed and delivered regularly?

- Is the execution being pictured as a whole or a short-term partial goal?

Are cycle times measured and reviewed to identify delays in delivery?

- Are we continuously identifying leaders apart from managers and contributors? Do people agree with the leaders who are appointed for them? Are these leaders capable of servant leadership? Are they in alignment with conscious leadership styles?

- How are we preventing burnout?

- Does our own workforce like the processes in the company? Are these processes balanced?

- Is there a process to monitor and minimize rework across teams?

- Are we constantly learning and improving? Does our work align with the mission and vision goal we had which we promised? Like my reviewer pointed out rightly, this is the most important aspect of growth. Is there a feedback mechanism in place? At all levels of execution?

- Most importantly, are we following the Agile Manifesto? What can we learn from the seven wastes of Lean software development?

Problem Details: We shall now take a deep dive and explain the problems. Quick reminder: Always inspect which Agile Manifesto principle might be compromised, especially when encountering challenges, to ensure alignment with core agile values and principles.

Context Switching Overload

When you're responding on multiple communication channels (Figma, Email, JIRA, Slack, Teams) for multiple projects, you're constantly reloading information in your brain with an updated context. Your focus is hardly where it should be – the technical correctness of the product. I have seen extremely capable team members lose their drive just because of context switching overload, and it is sad if everything in your company is fine and just because of communication channels, you lose out on good employees.

Context switching also leads to lesser time for deep work, which means lesser mastery. Which in turn leads to lesser motivation. If you do a cross-check with lean thinking, you'll realize that the number of communication paths and the substance communicated therein would ultimately lead to more waste than productivity. Research from MIT indicates that the human brain processes information at approximately 60 bits per second, highlighting the significant impact this limitation has on productivity, particularly in environments requiring constant multitasking. Humans perform best when focusing on one task at a time. Multitasking is a concept designed for processors, not people. We shouldn't expect humans to operate like computers in an attempt to keep pace with technology! Since there is little to no exposure to deep focus, there is **failure of mastery**.

Each context switch is a cost for the brain's finite processing capacity. Context switching overload is ultimately a brain injury, whether you like it or not. Increasing team frustration by mental fatigue with scattered communication is simply not the answer.

And which value of Agile is compromised here?

Individuals and interactions over processes and tools

—Agile Manifesto

You see, when the manifesto was signed, people were facing such problems as mentioned because of very similar reasons. The manifesto is just a Bible, as it is often called; it speaks of field experience, wisdom, and sensibility. Not understanding it will make you go through the same experience as the developers and then appreciate the value of it. Walk out of the circle, and adhere to the manifesto. Experience the solution and the magic, not the problems.

Focus on Reporting vs. Delivery

There is a clear antipattern when compared to the Agile Manifesto. Reporting is taking much of the employee's time and effort in the above scenario. This leads to *failure of purpose*. Failure of purpose leads to regret and loathing. You don't need that in your workforce. Take, for instance, the way the workforce is logging efforts and time. Micromanaging someone's time is highly discouraged. And that too, with a duplication of effort on three platforms? Understand why delivery teams would hate time logging, and trust me they do. A developer is tired after a day's work. He is not the one who is talking. He is the one who is thinking through code, probably working through someone's mess, and fixing bugs. A quality assurance team member needs to anticipate issues. He needs to see through branches of scenarios and maintain product health. If you tell these guys to maintain timesheets – and yes, you have every right to – then the least you can do for them is to not duplicate their effort. And in all this, what is being delivered is overlooked. Guess which values of Agile Manifesto are bypassed here?

> *Working software* over comprehensive documentation
>
> *Individuals and interactions* over processes and tools
>
> —Agile Manifesto

Again, if you focus so heavily on reporting, your focus on working software reduces, given a fixed team size. And if you increase the team size for more reporting, then managing that team won't be easy either.

Combining Product Owner and Scrum Master into One

Combining these two roles into one and calling this role as "Agile Project Manager" is a strange mistake that many, many companies make. There is a clear conflict of interest when these two roles collide into one. A single person acts as a proxy to the client and an advocate of the team. This means that the client loses a dedicated planner and reviewer and the team loses a dedicated advocate. This also leads to a single point of failure because of so many reasons – business use cases being written by, accounted for, and spearheaded in execution by this single manager add to implicit risks that cannot even be listed down. In the absence of this one person, the communication with the client and the team fails. The team too *may or may not be* self-organizing in the manager's absence. Since this manager works in different capacities, it is not practically possible for him to give autonomy to his team. As a Product Owner, he reviews their work – but as a Scrum Master, he steps back and facilitates their work. The moment the balance slips, it leads to **failure of autonomy**. Such managers, handling multiple projects both as Product Owner and Scrum Master for every project, complain of no work–life balance because most of their time is eaten up by work they did not sign up for. So, what went wrong here? It was the Scrum Guide that was not followed. Nowhere did the Scrum framework ask you to change or combine roles as you please. Such a manager is tired and exhausted. You expect two different sets of accountabilities from him, and you expect him to think like two opposing forces – sponsors and users on the one hand and developers on the other.

You cannot expect the efficiency of Scrum, if you don't follow it. And how was the manifesto compromised?

The best architectures, requirements, and designs emerge from self-organizing teams.

Agile processes promote sustainable development. The sponsors, developers, and users should be able to maintain a constant pace indefinitely.

—Agile Manifesto

The way I saw this scenario fail was that the manager nobody really looked into technical excellence of the product in such a case. The manager was busy in his split personality problem, thinking like the client, then thinking like the customer, then thinking like the senior management, then like the developer. The team wanted rest and lost its motivation, if this one manager was wrongly chosen.

Till here, we underlined three problems which not only were the antithesis of agile principles but also killed the famous three elements of motivation as listed by Dan Pink.

Autonomy, Mastery, and Purpose: It is the lack of these three elements that lead to the problem of demotivated, exhausted teams with sad energy. Nobody wanted to work in that unit. And everyone wondered why! Well, moving on to the most serious problems in my opinion.

Lack of Demos

This is the most serious mistake in this scenario, and many companies think that organizing work in Sprints is the beginning and end of the Scrum framework. Agility demands visibility and a fail-fast approach, and Jeff Sutherland in many of his talks has emphasized the importance of visibility through demo-based Sprint Reviews. Companies that lack demos will lack visibility into what is happening and to what extent is a software working. Remember how we explained how linear frameworks failed. Lack of visibility led to frustration. Demos help you to discover bugs faster in the cycle of development, and thinking that demos add no value and verbal status exchanges are enough is the saddest way of business execution. The most important thing is that teams receive actionable feedback during demos, allowing for quick adjustments and reducing the risk of delivering features that don't meet requirements. You even get a real chance of removing impediments, making everything relevant and making the SDLC transparent. Moreover, showcasing progress gives the team a sense of accomplishment, boosting morale and reinforcing the value of their contributions. In the scenario, "inspection," "transparency," and "adaptation" – the three pillars of empiricism – were not given a chance. Hence, there was no transparency.

What agile principle was compromised here?

Our highest priority is to satisfy the customer through early and continuous delivery of valuable software.

—Agile Manifesto

Lack of Retrospectives

How can Scrum function without retrospectives? Honestly, I'm not sure – but that's what some teams are doing. There's no pause to reflect on what could have been improved or to recognize the team's strengths. You cannot overemphasize the importance of retrospectives, but those who dismiss them as a waste often lack introspection, and no amount of encouragement can change that. It has to come from within. Hence, I'll move to the next problem and take up retrospective templates in detail when I speak of the solutions of Scenario 1.

Which principle of the Agile Manifesto was ignored here?

At regular intervals, the team reflects on how to become more effective, then tunes and adjusts its behavior accordingly.

—Agile Manifesto

Choice of Team Structure

We explained the component-based team structure in Figure 5-1. Refer to it again, if you wish to. On the face of it, the Android component we described won't seem a problem. But when you see how it creates a communication map with other components, you'll see you're causing the communication blast not only by tools but also by your team structure, because this is how it scales up to an organization level, as shown in Figure 5-4.

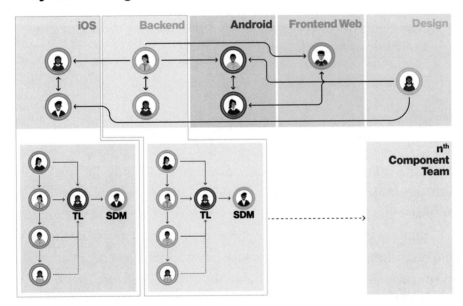

Figure 5-4. *The Existing Component Team Structure Resulting in a Typical Org Chart*

Org Charts are a strict no-no for agility, because they create too many pathways of communication and more chances of failing than streamlining performance. We shall see more in the section on Conway's Law.

In contrast, we have feature-based team structure. A feature-based team develops a feature, and who works on what platform is secondary. So, for the above scenario, any project dependent on design, back end, mobile, and front end could work feature wise. Microteams shown in Figure 5-5 could help.

Feature Based Teams

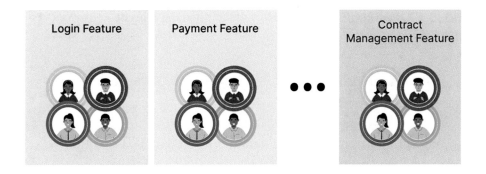

Build self sustaining teams that focus on vertically sliced features and not horizontally sliced components

Figure 5-5. *Feature-Based Teams*

Since your Sprint road map is divided into features, your microteams working on feature level are more intuitive. There are no handovers in this case, as compared to component-based teams that often work in silos. There is also more scope for deep focus. Plus, your team size will be a straightforward factor which influences how many features to take up in a Sprint.

If you look at how the teams are functioning in Scenario 1, you'll notice that these teams are operating in silos to a great extent. Even though an Android team collaborates with an iOS team and a back-end API team and so on, to make a product, their individual reporting to Android team leads and iOS team leads makes it into a knowledge silo problem. Component teams focus on their own platform and component, to hand it over to the person next in line. Their focus on the feature is much less in comparison to feature-oriented teams. Moreover, a component-based team often does not estimate correctly, regarding how many features they would deliver in a Sprint. It is much more intuitive when it is a feature-based team.

A knowledge silo problem results in too many indirect compromises with the Agile Manifesto. Here a few principles that suffer directly because of this challenge.

Continuous attention to technical excellence and good design enhances agility.

Agile processes promote sustainable development. The sponsors, developers, and users should be able to maintain a constant pace indefinitely.

Comparing feature-based and component-based teams, Table 5-1 provides a summary of feature comparison for both kinds of team structures.

Table 5-1. *Comparison between feature-based and component-based teams*

Feature	Component-Based Teams	Feature-Based Teams
Focus	Components or modules	End-to-end features
Structure	Technical or functional	Cross-functional
Ownership	Component-specific	Own the entire life cycle of a feature, from inception to delivery
Advantages	Deep expertise, reusability	Faster delivery, customer focus
Disadvantages	Silos, slower delivery	Needs to be restructured when scaled

While we introduced you to a scenario where component-based structure failed, for a real-life example of the success of feature-based teams, you'll need to wait till we introduce Conway's Law in this chapter. We'll tie the two concepts and it will make better sense.

Working Toward a Three-Fold Solution in Scenario 1

Let us work on a three-fold solution for the problems in Scenario 1. If you look at it from three broad aspects – following the Agile Manifesto, abiding by the framework, and lean thinking.

Following the Agile Manifesto

As we saw, the Agile Manifesto was compromised in every other challenge. For this purpose, you need an Agile Coach. We elaborate further:

Every organization needs an agile coach, who should stay and continuously drive agility and agile assessments within an organization. In many companies, it is thought that an agile coach is someone who introduces you to the Scrum and Kanban boards and walks off thereafter. An agile coach stays with you and revisits your implementation from time to time. A process consultant could be engaged from time to time to audit your implementation of work and agility toward the end results. The role of the agile coach is not the main theme of this book, but we will revisit agile assessments and agile metrics in the next chapter. That should help leaders to choose the right agile coach and mentor teams in an ongoing journey for agility.

A good agile coach would also help you to align your team with Lean Thinking, which is the next category of solutions we offer.

Alignment with Lean Thinking

- **Keep Balanced Documentation**: Remember that a stress on documentation over deliverables is not only against agile – it defeats lean. It causes waste.

- **Consolidate Communication Channels**: Keep everything in one or two tools only. Communication tools drive smoothness, and if we don't watch it when they get scattered, good talent will wither away with the chaos. I'd prefer JIRA and MS Teams.

- **Keep Focused Communication**: The actors in your framework should not mix up the purpose of calls from one to the other. What we mean is that it's easy to mix up standups and impediment resolution in the same call or Sprint Planning and previous Sprint Review in another. One meeting for a fixed purpose is the way to go.

Revisit the wastes of software development we discussed in Chapter 4 to understand why we keep stressing on lean thinking. Next, we offer solutions at the framework level, because many problems arose in this scenario when people did not abide by the framework.

Following the Scrum Guide

- **Scrum Accountabilities**: Separate the roles of Product Owner and Scrum Master.

- **Sprint Reviews**: Focus on demos instead of verbal Sprint Reviews.

- **Sprint Retrospectives:** Make Sprint Retrospectives a discipline that you enjoy and abide by.

Retrospective Philosophy

We briefly touched upon the OODA loop in Chapter 2, when we spoke of Jeff Sutherland's interview on the origin of Scrum. We understood how adaptation plays a key role in learning and continuous improvement.

Personally speaking, you don't need an Agile Manifesto to remind you that continuous improvement is the key for a successful life. You'd not become redundant, if you do not improve – but people around you would not like working with you. We promised retrospective templates earlier, but as the book progressed, I felt hat I should leave it to the reader to make templates but pen down a few questions that should lead to such templates:

1. What does the current approach lack?

2. What/who inspired me during this iteration?

3. Why couldn't we finish a particular task on time?

4. How could we improve our estimates? What did we learn from bad estimation?

5. Are we under undue pressure from the senior management?

6. How confident am I that I will not repeat my mistakes again?

7. Which mistakes did I repeat from the previous iterations?

8. What can I further improve in myself?

9. What are the key waste areas in our approach (Refer to Chapter 3 for a more exhaustive list on the kinds of waste, and identify more on your own):

   a. Waste related to time

   b. Waste related to dependency

   c. Waste related to partially done work

   d. Waste related to extra processes

   e. Waste related to lack of standardization

   f. ... and more

10. Where did we lack in (be careful in this question; we don't want one or two people to feel bad. Keep it realistic, soft, and acceptable. Give at the max one pointer in all or no areas):

    a. Management

    b. Quality control

    c. Development

    d. Design

11. What were my lessons?

12. What were the team's lessons?

13. Are we agile in behavior?

14. Are we contradicting the Scrum Guide, if following Scrum?

15. What can we learn from the Scrum Guide this time? Any new pointers?

16. What are similar products in the market about? Can we increase our domain knowledge about the product we are making?

17. Are we connected with business, or is the development progress not in alignment with long-term business vision?

18. What kind of compliances did we learn?

19. What were the challenges around deployment? Is deployment clashing with agility?

20. Is continuous integration being followed in practice?

21. What did we learn from resource allocation?

22. What were surprise areas for us in development?

23. Were distributed teams taken into account when the road map and timeline was shared?

24. Were any of the following time estimations considered when estimates were shared?

    a. Client meetings and discussions

    b. Formal reviews

    c. Tool maintenance

    d. Documentation effort

25.   Were we working on tried and tested technology, and were buffers added for tech spikes?

26.   Is the client psychology such that things can be kept negotiable, or is the client not agile himself?

27.   How was code review handled?

Retrospectives are ultimately a tool for introspection, and it's not just for the team as a whole – it's for questioning yourself. There can be no single template for continuous improvement. It's a life long journey of self-discovery.

Retrospectives are profound tools for personal and collective growth, transforming self-reflection into actionable insights. They are not about adhering to rigid templates but about cultivating a continuous, individualized approach to learning and improvement throughout one's life journey.

The essence of a meaningful retrospective is holding yourself accountable. Be careful not to play blame games. Transforming self-reflection into actionable insights is not always easy, but if you keep it in mind, you do achieve appreciation and understanding of the situation at hand.

Apart from the above most obvious ones, there are some other pointers that need to be introduced, and the first and most important is the Conway's Law.

Conway's Law

Conway's Law, named after computer programmer Melvin Conway, *states that organizations tend to design systems that mirror their own communication structures.* In other words, how a team is organized and how it communicates will influence the design of the product or system they create.

Refer to Figures 5-1, 5-2, and 5-4, which discuss an individual component, components at a team level, and components at a project level. The communication pathways in the organization because of such a structure would be immense. Here's how.

Reiterating the team structure and communication pathways here, you see that within a project,

1. There are components of iOS, Back End, Android, Front End Web, and Design (Figure 5-2).

2. Backend APIs feed into iOS, Front End Web, and Android.

3. Design feeds into all teams except for Back-End APIs (there might be a possibility when this might occur too).

4. The QA component takes feed from all components.

5. The number of communication pathways for such a team, irrespective of a common standup or Scrum call, is immense. Scale this to multiple teams and projects. There is no limit to the way your teams are communicating.

6. Another problem in Scenario 1 was that all iOS developers, probably ten in number, were reporting to a single iOS component lead who would, among other things, train them, evaluate them, understand user stories for them, guide tech spikes on newer trends and research, and much more. There was very little room for this iOS lead to grow on his own. The poor tech leads remained on calls day in and day out. Meeting to meeting to meeting. Hence, it was not just the waste due to

communication – it was the team structure that
caused the waste. All team leads were then reporting
to the Senior Delivery Manager (refer to Figure 5-4).
The communication pathways for a single person
again were multidimensional. Fortunately, or
unfortunately, I have been part of such systems,
and I know now how communication should not be
handled.

Coming back to Conway's Law, the number of pathways is bound to
degrade the quality of the solutions built. As your organization scales, it is
going to cause more problems. See Figure 5-6.

Figure 5-6. *The Problem with the Existing Team Structure*
When Scaled
Image source: Atlassian

My proposed team structure is as shown in Figure 5-7. Segregated
teams working on different clients turned out to be more cost-effective and
easier to track. A Scrum of Scrums could wrap around these client-
oriented teams as an industry standard solution to track how these Scrum
Teams were performing at an individual level.

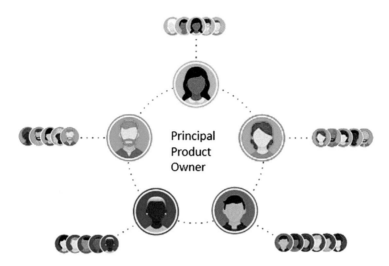

Figure 5-7. *Individual Scrum Masters for all Projects Reporting to the Principal Product Owner*
Image courtesy: Atlassian

However, there should be no need for individual teams to regularly communicate with each other as part of a process, as if they were components. This in effect reduces the context switching for managers since the number of times they are communicating and the purpose of communication is more well defined and limited. If you see one level deep, your demos in this team design will be more contextual because they will be related to the project team that is closely tied to each other. Dig deeper; each team when combined with a feature-based team topology will deliver faster within and will be self-sustainable. For instance, the team working for Client 1 will be working on demos for Client 1. They have nothing to do with demos of Client 2. Earlier, in the org chart we showed you, the Team Lead for Back End was overseeing operations in all projects, all clients. Now, the tech lead if you wish to appoint one (not needed by Scrum) will be accountable for only the projects that he is working on.

All this might just appear to be theory, and it's not necessary that this will suit your organization – but it has a better chance than the team structure we showed in Scenario 1.

The problem comes when you combine this approach randomly with any approach, **without thinking it through. I repeat, without thinking it through.** For instance, if you somehow like the concept of saviors, you can't just plug it in with the team structure suggested above. Your principle of team topology should be to achieve value with minimal waste. And this in effect means that when you do introduce a demonstration-based culture as directed in Scrum, you should have a very straightforward way of doing it. If that isn't happening, there is something amiss. Earlier, your demonstration either didn't happen at all, or if introduced, you'd have to demonstrate to your peers in the same team, the delivery manager, the Scrum Master, and the team lead. By keeping a consolidated and decoupled team structure with high cohesion, we get a five-fold benefit to say in the least:

- **Consolidated Communication**: Communication happens per project or client.

- **Autonomous Teams**: When teams know that they are accountable to the client and not to internal hierarchies, they become more autonomous. You see self-organization and no dependency on team leads as in the existing model.

- **Improved Decision-Making**: Autonomy adds to better decision-making.

- **Increased Focus on the Customer**: Cross-functional work can happen better in decoupled teams than in endless communication.

- **Modular Design**: Alan D. MacCormack, who is well known for his research in the management of innovation and new product development, with a focus on the design and deployment of digital technologies, reveals the benefits of agile processes and the value of modular designs, when he says in his work that "an architecture for participation that promotes ease of understanding by limiting module size...." By keeping things team sized, you are inadvertently promoting participating and modular design. Whenever you draw out your team structure, you should be wary of organizational charts because they'll hardly pay off and make matters more complex. Instead, focus on how individual teams prosper and nourish. It changes perspective.

Now, this example was a very simple citation from a software setup. You'll find the same problem resonating even in industries that are inherently complex – like the construction industry. If contractors and subcontractors work in silos, you'll have cost overruns, miscommunication, and inaccessible results. Silos, component-based structures, and bad communication paths are a result of company culture. People who respect collaboration will ultimately find a way. People who play for jobs, or power or short cuts and the like, will not form efficient communication pathways, and their app design will suffer.

Restructuring teams and organization to set the communication channels to the way you want the architecture to go is called a "Inverse Conway's maneuver," and interested readers should check work and material on this by **Martin Fowler**. As he says in his articles, this is not an all-powerful system, but is a good start, if you are in the middle of a messy team structure and your communication patterns are baffling.

If you understood Conway's Law and its applicability to Scenario 1, you are good to go with an exploration about more team structures and why they fail and succeed. Now, we'll keep a few old promises.

We promised you a case study where we'll give a real-life success story of Conway's Law. Here it is.

Case Study: Unix – A Success in Conway's Law

Unix was created by a group of programmers at Bell Labs in the 1960s and 1970s. The group was organized into small, autonomous teams, each responsible for a specific part of the operating system. This decentralized structure led to the development of a modular system, made up of many small, independent components that could be easily combined to form larger applications. This modularity and flexibility were a direct result of the way the development team was organized. The decentralized structure of the team encouraged the development of independent components that could be easily reused and combined in different ways. This made Unix a highly adaptable and versatile operating system, which contributed to its widespread adoption and success.

The Unix example illustrates how Conway's Law can have a positive impact on system design. By organizing teams in a way that mirrors the desired system architecture, it is possible to create systems that are more modular, flexible, and adaptable.

However, Conway's Law can also have negative consequences. If a team is organized in a way that does not reflect the desired system architecture, it can lead to the development of systems that are difficult to maintain, extend, and evolve. It is important to be aware of Conway's Law and to consider how team organization can impact system design. By carefully designing teams and communication structures, it is possible to create systems that are more likely to be successful and meet the needs of users.

Here's a good read: Conway's Law: the little-known principle that influences your work more than you think.

Such examples show you that when people put their mind to team design, they make everyone's life easy. The book *Team Topologies* by Matthew Skelton and Manuel Pais describes the same point but on a much deeper level. It makes for a great read. You should certainly read that book if you feel your organization is suffering from bad team design, as it takes you through Stream-Aligned Teams (similar to feature-based teams like we described.), Platform Teams (teams build and maintain platforms that enable other teams to deliver value more efficiently), Complicated Subsystem Teams (responsible for maintaining and improving intricate parts of the system that are generally unchanging, like one for handling financial transactions), and Enabling Teams (support and expertise to other teams, such as in areas like architecture, security, or data science), among a wealth of more knowledge. The main idea is to align team boundaries with the flow of work and the need for specialized teams to address specific domains of complexity. This is where Scenario 1 failed really: If you want your tech leads to do everything under the Sun and multitask, and you are combining roles, you cannot expect outcome or output. The book also emphasizes the importance of context-driven decision-making in choosing the appropriate team topology for a given situation. It also highlights the need for continuous adaptation and evolution of team structures as the organization's needs and challenges change over time.

When we started talking about what makes a framework, we mentioned actors, team structures, artifacts, values, events, and purposeful abstraction.

We took up a scenario and inspected the role of actors and team structures could have improved this scenario and how communication pathways played an important role in the same. We now move on to artifacts.

Artifacts

Artifacts represent work or value. They can be anything ranging from models, prototypes, workflow diagrams, design documents, and setup scripts to Product Backlog (Work Breakdown Structure), Sprint Backlog (in the case of Scrum), and Increment (or goal in the case of Scrum). Actors work with artifacts. The key to having good artifacts is to see what represents value and how balanced they are in number.

Interestingly, in the summer of 2023, I interviewed for a very large organization in software development and here's what they said – "Are you good at documentation? We follow standards and our project managers complain that it is too much for them. We don't want balanced documentation; we want heavy documentation...." Fortunately, for me, I was not selected. Moving on, let us place artifacts in a scenario and see how this comes along in the whole picture.

Scenario 2: AZIT Pvt Ltd

Imagine a unit where artifacts were not seen as representatives of value (again, I have seen it happening recently, with a client of mine). Things that were marked of value were not associated with business vision. Some prominent markers in this scenario were as follows:

1. There were numerous interconnected healthcare projects, which were in different stages of development. These were maintained under versions. While working on version 3, deliverables from version 1 were also left unaddressed and unlabeled on JIRA.

2. Because of the lack of labelling on JIRA, there was difficulty in locating relevant information.

3. There was an information overload because of the nature of the domain – healthcare. There were hundreds of Medicare contracts with their different types and privileges. Role management and authorization was a mess, and at the end of many Sprints, the developers were left confused about business logic despite user stories. The user stories were coupled and not cohesive.

4. Crucial acceptance criteria were missing.

5. The design prototypes did not make for good workflows and edge cases.

6. On JIRA, features, epics, user stories, and tasks do not seem to make canonical sense. For instance, for every business use case, there were two kinds of stories:

   a. Business user story.

   b. Back-end service story.

   c. These were related to each other on JIRA.

7. The developers were asked to log in time with hours. If the logged efforts exceeded estimates, developers were held accountable by the client team. That built pressure on the teams developing.

8. With every ticket was a field called stack order, which was meant to prioritize the tickets in a way that development could proceed smoothly. **Reprioritization of the backlog was not permitted by the client.** So, the team ran into an issue, where the stack order of edit user was, say, 101, and search user was 102. The only place where the end user could have entered into the edit user screen was via the search user results. Something like the grid shown in Figure 5-8, where the developers were not left with an entry point on the user interface for edit user because of incorrect stack order.

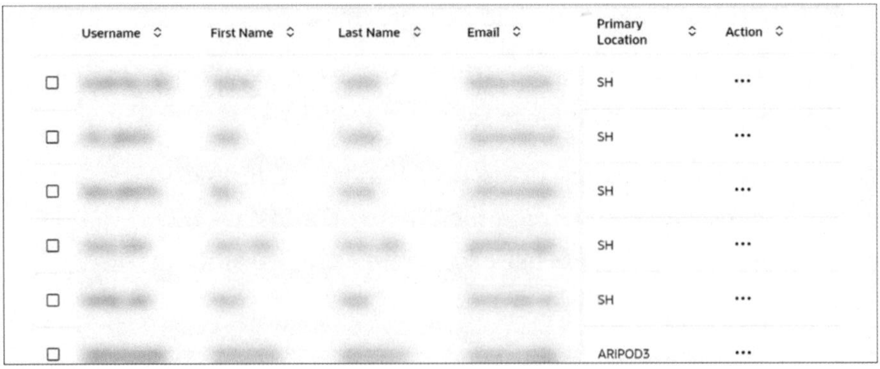

Username ⇕	First Name ⇕	Last Name ⇕	Email ⇕	Primary Location ⇕	Action ⇕
☐				SH	⋯
☐				SH	⋯
☐				SH	⋯
☐				SH	⋯
☐				SH	⋯
☐				ARIPOD3	⋯

Figure 5-8. *Incorrect Prioritization Can Lead to Insensible Execution of the Backlog*

9. At the end of the Sprint, there was an (n-1) Sprint testing. So, you'd handover a Sprint, and a client acceptance test would begin for that particular Sprint. It was called an (n-1) Sprint test, because in Sprint 3, the client would be testing Sprint 2. If a Sprint would not be handed over for client testing on time, there were heated calls.

10. During estimation, code review was never considered as part of the estimations. Code review was delayed by the client regularly, and PRs were slow.

11. There was only one environment which was provided, and that wasn't ready till the middle of the third Sprint. This environment was available to all for testing – the service provider's QA, the client QA, and the service provider's developers.

12. The team managed to deliver somehow, but five months later, when another team wanted to execute the same project, crucial artifacts were not in place, and the new Product Owner did not know the source of truth – the deliverable or the user stories (which were incomplete and were not properly sliced across features and epics).

Problem Identification in Scenario 2

Anyone would tell you what the problem was in Scenario 2.

1. **Define Value**

   - For a system of interconnected projects where there some versions are redundant, artifacts need refiltering and regular cleanup. So how were lean principles defeated here? Waste was not identified.

   - The lack of relevant information at the right time leads to waste, again an antipattern for lean.

   - Visual aids like prototypes help many developers remember a workflow by complementing words with prototype navigation. If an edge case is covered through visual design, it adds real value. However, adding too many test cases as workflows, prematurely, is also not of value. The keyword is balance. Crucial acceptance criteria should be included in sync, for developers to understand what business needs are. Whatever isn't of value is ultimately a waste.

2. **Lack of Technical Excellence**: Acceptance criteria define the definition of done for developers. Missing the acceptance criteria is a risk you would not want to take in complex business logic. You are also not following Scrum.

   Which Agile Manifesto principle do you think was defeated here?

   I'd say:

   Continuous attention to technical excellence enhances agility

   —Agile Manifesto

3. **Horizontal Instead of Vertical Slicing:** The team has apparently followed horizontal slicing. Splitting user stories through horizontal slicing (taking a feature and splitting it by components such as back end, front end, and API) is incorrect. A user story is ultimately what is delivered to the end user. And it should be sliced vertically – with user stories that define business logic only. So, for a business story that requires the user to, say, associate a Medicare contract with a user, you should not split this into Back-End Story, API Story, and Front-End Story. It should be a single business user story related to the contract association as a business need. Figure 5-9 shows the same point, to demonstrate the difference between horizontal and vertical slicing.

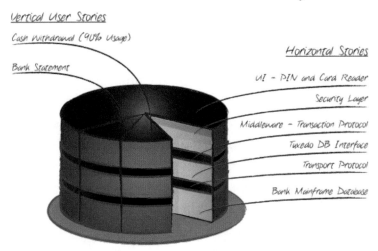

Figure 5-9. *Horizontal and Vertical User Stories*
Image source: Delta Matrix

The main drawbacks of horizontal slicing are as follows:

- It leads to the lack of optimization of workflow because your developers end up estimating multiple user stories, instead of estimating the complexity of one feature. In contrast, if you develop user stories according to features, your team will maintain a sustainable pace of development. As a result, the team moves towards the product goal at a comfortable pace, knowing what features have been developed, rather than tracking what interfaces (database, UI, backend, network) have been developed. The manifesto says the same:

Agile processes promote sustainable development. The sponsors, developers, and users should be able to maintain a constant pace indefinitely.

—Agile Manifesto

143

- It leads to waste, because your Scrum Team and Product Owner and Scrum Master need to look at three user stories instead of one, for every vertical slice shown above.

- The feedback loop is lengthened with horizontal slicing because each layer (e.g., back end, front end, API) is developed independently and in isolation, delaying the creation of a fully functional, testable feature. Vertical slicing creates a **narrow, functional feature** (end-to-end) that can be demonstrated, tested, and refined early in the process. Feedback on usability, business value, and functionality is immediate, enabling quicker iterations. Testing cannot begin effectively until all layers are combined into a cohesive feature.

The principle being compromised here is:

Delivering value to the customer early and continuously

—Agile Manifesto

- Also, keep in mind that the technical implementation is something that should be defined by the developers. So again, in effect, you are not aligned with Scrum. Primarily, because your way of understanding the backlog is not customer centric. Instead, you are focusing on "how" it should be implemented by developers.

Primarily because the feedback loop is lengthened but also because artifacts are not considered as measure of value, but of number.

4. **Coupling Over Cohesion:** Even during vertical slicing, business user stories should not be coupled. Instead, using the INVEST principle (described later in this book), you should focus on decoupled stories. Horizontal slicing is inevtiably going to lead to coupled user stories, which all depend on each other for completion. For instance, if you make stories on front end integration, backend integration, database - all connected to the same feature - all stories will be coupled - and not cohesive. The INVEST principle we discuss later, overcomes this easily.

5. **Killing Autonomy:**

   - Micromanagement of hours and the pressure around it is also not an agile way of software development. It reduces trust and creates a hindrance in executing Scrum, because you are devaluing collaboration. Again, Scrum values are at stake.

   Whenever you kill autonomy, the one common principle that you bypass is:

Build projects around motivated individuals. Give them the environment and support they need, and trust them to get the job done.

—Agile Manifesto

6. **Framework Level Flaws:** The failure to embrace **backlog prioritization, refinement,** and **continuous testing** undermines agility, compromising the team's ability to adapt to change, deliver value incrementally, and maintain technical excellence. Moreover, (n-1) tests have not been defined by Scrum. This shows the purpose of writing this book. Many companies tweak Scrum to suit their purpose, not realizing the implications behind it. The Scrum Guide spoke of an

Increment, and if the Increment is not achieved, the definition of done is not met. You cannot time box the testing effort into a Sprint succeeding the previous one.

7. **Lack of Flow:** Lack of environments to deploy and test smoothly shows devaluing technical excellence – it reduces optimum flow. Deployment is a full topic in itself, and the least you could do for your team is to provide them with a common environment to create optimum workflow. We touch upon some best practices for deployment such as Continuous Integration vs. Feature Branching and the wiser approach to take, when we talk of CI/CD in the next chapter.

8. **Failing Agile and Lean Both:** By failing to account for indirect activities such as PR approvals, environment not being set up, and effort on test case documentation – bottlenecks arise. This not only results in wasted time, inefficient workflows, and a slower delivery process but also shows lack of transparency, while making the road map is a factor that will have its consequences on the timeline.

Keep in mind that your processes and tools should undervalue working software. Delays in PR is a hindrance to agility because you are not delivering continuously for the customer.

If your test case documentation is so extensive that the Scrum Team and Product Owners are buried under it, then it's a demotivator for the team, because it reduces focus on the working software.

We repeat the emphasis on various principles and values of the Agile Manifesto:

Our highest priority is to satisfy the customer through the early and continuous delivery of valuable software.

Working software is the primary measure of progress.

Deliver working software frequently, from a couple of weeks to a couple of months, with a preference to the shorter timescale.

Individuals and interactions over processes and tools

Working software over comprehensive documentation

It's no joke. People will continue to suffer, without anyone's ill intention, if you create antipatterns of agility,

In each of the points described in the problem identification sections, we provided a solution. Basically, see if you are creating an antipattern in agility, and go back to see the impact. The solution will come by reversing the antipattern and following Lean and Agile. The two should not be isolated from each other in philosophy.

Planning an Artifact and Breaking It Down

We saw how badly planned artifacts can create a mess. It's worth mentioning that the Scrum way of maintaining timely artifacts is possibly the best that the industry has seen.

- Product Backlog

- Sprint Backlog

- Increment

Breaking down your requirement into the Product Backlog, represented by epics, user stories, tasks, and features (or whichever format of representation you might like), is a must, provided your breakdown makes canonical sense and is vertical. Writing good user stories is covered in detail in the section called "INVEST in Good User Stories," and breaking down units of deliverables into artifacts of value is covered next. Not being able to identify whether your user stories are relevant or not can be achieved through good labelling and data organization on a project management tool. If the Scrum Master and Product Owner are not meticulous regarding this, a hard call needs to be taken to avoid this.

Let us deep dive into how the Product Backlog should be broken down considering an example of the healthcare domain. This example was very similar to the problem described in the scenario above, because the number of features and compliances associated made the business logic difficult to understand in a few places.

The main problem statement was that the company extended Medicare contracts to many clients in the United States. The management of those contracts was the issue that they wanted to address, with proper authorization and association to users. In this section, we break down this system into epics, features, and user stories since this is a popular format which is used with Scrum for Product Backlog items.

Consider Table 5-2, which speaks of the epics, features, and user stories of such a system. Notice how the slicing is done vertically and not horizontally.

Table 5-2. *Artifact planning in the form of epics, features, and user stories*

Epic	Feature	User Stories
User management		
	Create user	
		Create user
	Assign user permissions	
		Assign user permissions as super admin for a sub admin
		Assign user permissions by super admin for another super admin

(continued)

Table 5-2. (*continued*)

Epic	Feature	User Stories
Authorization		
	Permissions for portal access	
		Super admin permissions
		Sub admin permissions
Authentication		
	Portal access	
		Logging in
		Logging out
	MF authentication	
		Reset MFA
		Add MFA
	Unlock/lock authentication	
		Unlock authentication by super admin
		Lock authentication by super admin
		Unlock authentication by sub admin
		Lock authentication by sub admin

(*continued*)

Table 5-2. (*continued*)

Epic	Feature	User Stories
Role group management		
	Create role group	
		Create role group by super admin
		Create role group by sub admin
	Edit role group	
		Edit role group by super admin
		Edit role group by sub admin
	Delete role group	
		Delete role group by super admin
		Delete role group by sub admin
Contract management		
	Contract association with role group and user	
		Contract association with role group and super admin user
		Contract association with role group and sub admin user

First, let us understand how we are vertically slicing epics, features, and user stories.

An epic is a large body of work that spans multiple Sprints (or iterations).

A feature is a single feature to be deployed with groups of related functions. Ideally, I would choose one feature to be the size of one Sprint. The hierarchy is simple: Epics ➤ feature ➤ user story. The definition is simpler. A user story is a single business function, which when grouped with other stories makes a feature.

Up to here, our example describes the title of epics, features, and user stories. How are they described? Let us start with the description format of a user story.

As a <persona>, I need to <business function>, so that I can <business purpose>

INVEST in Good User Stories

The quality of a user story matters because it is one of the primary artifacts through which you communicate business value. A good user story is accompanied by acceptance criteria which go on to become its definition of done and is written with certain criteria in mind. Let's dig deeper into the INVEST principle through Figure 5-10.

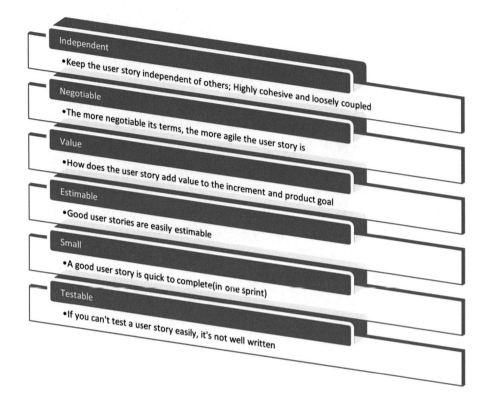

Independent
• Keep the user story independent of others; Highly cohesive and loosely coupled

Negotiable
• The more negotiable its terms, the more agile the user story is

Value
• How does the user story add value to the increment and product goal

Estimable
• Good user stories are easily estimable

Small
• A good user story is quick to complete(in one sprint)

Testable
• If you can't test a user story easily, it's not well written

Figure 5-10. *Writing a Good User Story with INVEST*

We shall now use the above story titles and attempt to describe them using INVEST as a torch in Listing 5-1.

Listing 5-1. A sample description for a user story for portal permissions

User Story Title: Assign User Permissions by Super Admin for another Super Admin

User Story Description:
As a super admin,

I want to assign specific permissions (Delete User, Reset MFA, Add MFA, View Contracts, and Associate Contracts) to other super admins,
so that they have the appropriate access to perform required actions.

The user story only speaks of assignment of user permissions to Super Admin. It does not take up any associated function. This makes it independent. The user story is negotiable, because you can easily add to the user permissions and subtract from the list. If, however, you add a line like "*These permissions cannot be changed or altered once the system is developed and deployed*," then you are making business needs nonnegotiable. The system back fires then. The user story adds value to the product goal, because it is a key feature to be implemented. The user story is estimable. The implementation of this user story is clear enough to be estimated. The task can be broken down into manageable technical components, such as the permission interface, assignment logic, and audit logging. The user story is small. It's not as if developers cannot complete the assignment of these permissions to a user, based on privilege in one Sprint. The user story is testable; if you had added a line like "*Permissions can only be added once a month*," you'd be creating a difficult to test user story, because nothing can be tested once a month.

Developing good user stories is not only the responsibility of Product Owners; it is also the responsibility of the entire Scrum Team. That is why backlog grooming is an important activity in Scrum.

The acceptance criteria of such a user story could look something like in Listing 5-2.

Listing 5-2. An Example of Writing Acceptance Criteria

```
Scenario: See list of permissions to be assigned
    Given I am logged in as a super admin
    When I navigate to the "Permissions Management" page
    Then I should see a list of all super administrators
```

```
And I should see a list of available permissions:
    | Delete User        |
    | Reset MFA          |
    | Add MFA            |
    | View Contracts     |
    | Associate Contracts|

Scenario: Validation for no permissions selected
    Given I am on the "Permissions Management" page
    And I deselect all permissions for a super administrator
    When I click the "Save" button
    Then I should see an error message "At least one permission
    must be assigned."
```

We've now seen how artifacts can be broken down and planned and what makes a good artifact. We have also seen what can happen when value is not attached to the right artifact at the right time. Let us now talk of risks attached to a given framework.

Scenario 3

Addressing Risk Management in Any Given Framework

The reason why we address this topic now is because while planning and deciding artifacts in your framework, many teams forget or underrate risks. Unfortunately, the Scrum Guide does not speak of risk management during planning explicitly nor does Kanban visualization. These being the two major frameworks that people follow in agile methods, the entire risk-oriented mindset gets overlooked sometimes. However, it's not that the creators of the Scrum method or Kanban did not offer implicit ways to handle risk. Risk management gets implicitly handled through customer feedback in agile. Shorter iterations and more demos lead to greater identification of the problem at hand rather than planning for risks and then leaving them on the shelf.

The custom framework that you are planning, however, could identify categories of risks per artifact. Here's an interesting example I found from one of my projects.

I was an agile coach for a customer support system that had hundreds of tickets in a month. There was no system, barring a simple email to JIRA automation, where the end customer of the system could simply shoot an email to the product manager and a corresponding ticket would be logged in JIRA. There was no filtering where we could understand the nature of issues that the end users were facing. To add to the complexity of the situation, the app being used relied heavily on a third-party system which had to be contacted every time an issue was reported. Ultimately, after a year of solving issues, the board was still overflowing with hundreds of unresolved tickets with no idea about what they contain. There was simply no process at all, and people were overworked. The application in question had a good architectural diagram in place. The staff working on issues had good domain knowledge, but nobody ever had enough time left to think.

Here are some examples of questions that leaders could have asked themselves before stepping into a project with no process at all:

Financial Risks

- How might inefficient issue resolution processes lead to increased operational costs?

- What is the potential financial impact of customer dissatisfaction on sales and revenue?

- How might the use of third-party connectors in the ticketing system impact operational costs, particularly in terms of licensing fees, maintenance, and integration efforts?

- What are the potential financial risks associated with relying on third-party vendors for critical components of the ticketing system, such as security, data privacy, or performance?

Operational Risks

- Could the lack of a reliable ticketing system result in service disruptions, especially during peak usage times?

- How could the absence of a centralized knowledge base impact operational efficiency and support costs?

- What are the potential compliance risks associated with human error in a manual ticketing system, particularly for organizations subject to industry-specific regulations?

- How could the integration of third-party connectors into the ticketing system increase the complexity of operations and maintenance?

- How might the use of third-party connectors impact the organization's ability to respond quickly to security threats or data breaches?

Once you set aside time to ask yourself such questions, you tend to build a robust execution system where your main artifacts are well handled. Here, the artifacts were not the usual Product Backlog items, and they would come at any time of the day, week, or month. Planning was obviously not straightforward, but does that mean that the artifact should lack risk identification? No. In fact, no matter what framework you use, spend some time on risk registers, for yourself. You don't have to kill yourselves with the load of elaborate risk response plans or risk dashboards unless you need them, but you'd see that you eliminate a lot of potential hurdles with clients. Remember to keep everything lean. ***What's not adding value, needs to be eliminated.*** The case described above accumulated a lot of waste, which was difficult to handle by the time it piled up. Ultimately any scenario that goes wrong lacks a lean or agile approach. No matter what framework you choose, it's the principles we discussed earlier in the book that should be kept in mind.

Artifacts cannot be understated in any agile setup. It's ultimately that what you operate on. We asked a set of 50 capable industry leaders about the challenges in execution of projects and subsequent review. Figure 5-11 provides the survey results.

Figure 5-11. *Survey Results for Challenges in Project Execution*

Engineers and leaders apparently could handle most things but a poorly defined backlog and bad Sprint Planning. That should tell you the importance of artifacts such as a backlog. And as far as planning is concerned, you'd want to create events in your framework which are carefully sorted out for your team and not just the organization's process.

Events

Every framework will require events for execution. Operational success comes with a lot of practice, and sadly, for some organizations, it comes and disappears with wrong choices, lack of value systems, oversight, or lack of motivation – or a thousand odd reasons. The intention of this section is not to lay down the exact events that your framework should have but what you should keep in mind during framing those events as an acceptable procedure for your team.

One important factor is the cognitive workload that your team members can take up with efficiency. Let's see what cognitive workload is, and we'll look at Scenario 1 of this chapter to see how lack of adherence to the same led to problems.

Addressing Cognitive Workload

Cognitive workload refers to the mental effort and resources required to perform a specific task or activity. It's essentially a measure of how demanding a particular task is on an employee's brain. John Sweller characterized it as the total amount of mental effort being used in the working memory.

Here are some key factors that contribute to cognitive workload:

- **Task Complexity:** More complex tasks, involving multiple steps, decision-making, or problem-solving, generally increase cognitive workload.

- **Information Overload:** When employees are bombarded with too much information at once, their cognitive capacity can become overwhelmed.

- **Time Pressure:** Working under tight deadlines can add stress and increase cognitive demands.

- **Interruptions:** Frequent interruptions can disrupt the flow of work and make it more difficult to maintain focus.

- **Task Novelty:** New or unfamiliar tasks may require more cognitive effort as employees learn and adapt.

- **Individual Factors:** Personal differences, such as cognitive abilities, experience, and stress levels, can also influence how demanding a task feels.

- **Assumption of Zero Cognitive Load:** Often, when new work is allocated, managers assume that an employee has zero cognitive workload. In effect, it is taken for granted that the working memory from project/task 1 is nullified, as soon as the employee should switch to the next project/task. Add to it cost management – and the result is a disaster and burnt-out employees.

All of these points can become questions that leaders need to ask themselves before, during, and after a project is finished.

- Is the workload evenly distributed among team members? Are there individuals carrying too much or too little? Do a survey, if it helps.

- Are tasks aligned with individual strengths and interests? This can help to reduce cognitive overload and increase motivation.

- Are there opportunities for task simplification or automation? Reducing the complexity of tasks can alleviate cognitive load. For example, JIRA automation for status reporting is often underestimated in startups, and the resulting reporting limbo placed on managers is a direct consequence of this oversight.

- Are there clear communication channels and processes in place? Effective communication can reduce confusion and prevent misunderstandings.

- Are team members encouraged to collaborate and seek help when needed? This can prevent individuals from feeling overwhelmed.

- Are there opportunities for knowledge sharing and learning? Sharing knowledge can reduce cognitive load for individuals and the team as a whole.

- How can we ensure team members have dedicated time for focused tasks to enhance memory retention and facilitate deep work?

Events are based on activities that are considered important for project completion. Scrum creates events around planning, reporting, review, and reflection. You can take your pick, but more or less, your events will circle the same activities too. Remember to keep lean thinking and agile in mind though. Eliminate waste, above all, because it's through daily activities and artifacts that major waste accumulates.

What's most important is the culture that surrounds events. A lot of that depends on values, but the best of people face problems in meetings which we shall now cover. A more conscious effort by leaders to stay away from these biases will help improve meetings and collaboration. Let's start with lack of self-reflection, because this one problem covers everything else. It was not for nothing that retros were introduced in Scrum. We spoke of the power of retrospectives in Chapter 3, and we can only reemphasize it here. Agility stands on the pillar of continuous reflection and learning. Leaders who lead will need to self-reflect and lead. Let us now take a look at one key human behavior that influences all events in a team: bias.

Identifying Bias

Communication, work, and perceptions are clouded by every day biases, and more often than not, work takes a back seat and human behavioral challenges keep coming across. The sad fact, however, is that human behavioral challenges will keep facing you every step of the way. Is it really worthwhile to lose a part of yourself because of someone's behavior?

Speaking of bias, here's a very rudimentary list of biases that I have discovered on close observation in meetings and events that were meant to handle execution. These biases took away the whole charm of work, but there they are. An ugly truth. After listing them, we'll see if they start within or externally.

> **Anchoring Bias:** This occurs when people rely too heavily on the first piece of information they encounter when making decisions. For example, a manager might set an unrealistic sales target based on a previous year's performance, leading to unnecessary stress and frustration. Another common anchor bias is to pick one star employee and without understanding what he's good at give him every single thing. I've seen that happen everywhere in the software technology sector at least. It makes you sad, but there it is – it glares us in the face.

> **Priority Bias:** This bias involves judging the likelihood of an event based on how easily examples come to mind. For instance, a company might prioritize addressing a problem that has recently made headlines, even if it's a relatively minor issue. This happened with a client who wanted weekly statuses above everything else. The company just magically reset its focus to status updates, and everything else lost balance. Not to my surprise, the client who was not agile in the first place, and the company that didn't value agility, didn't get along well for too long.

Confirmation Bias: People tend to seek out information that confirms their existing beliefs and avoid information that contradicts them. This can lead to groupthink and hinder the ability to make objective decisions. If your events are suffering from actors' participation who seek validation, you know there's a problem, and you'll have to fix it.

Groupthink: This occurs when a group of people prioritize consensus over critical thinking. It can lead to poor decision-making and a lack of creativity. I've seen this happen right in front of my eyes so many times. The silliest episode was when an estimate of three hours was exaggerated to three days because of groupthink. The task really just needed three hours! The ones who were right were outnumbered by the ones who were technically incorrect. The ones who prioritized consensus over critical thinking eventually had their say.

In-group/Out-group Bias: People tend to favor members of their own group and be prejudiced against members of other groups. This can lead to discrimination and hinder collaboration. Always a human condition, isn't it?

Hierarchical Bias: This occurs because of hierarchy in organizations and can surface in many ways. When a group of people prioritize a team lead's decision without voicing an honest opinion, it's a straight example of hierarchical bias. It can lead to poor decision-making and a lack of creativity. I've seen this happen right in front of my eyes so many times. People can flock with a superior and nod to what he says. End of story!

There are plenty more biases out there, ready to creep in. It's for us to watch out and stay at bay. How often we are able to do it determines how often we are able to be good facilitators and leaders, good team players, and good product developers. The trick is to not let people be judged by who they are perceived to be. To raise your team's awareness would be a good start before you jump into the project. Orientation, conflict management, environment checks, and the like are all understated and should be visited and revisited from time to time. We check these concepts again when we visit the value system, but we'll couple it with Plutchik's Wheel of Emotions to add color to our point. But till then, it's safe to remember that any contingency is a two-way street to solve. And mostly, if you are facing a challenge in your team, it starts with you, and then, it becomes a collective effort to solve it. Leadership has never been and cannot be a one-person show. Building teams that trust each other is the best measure of human success that you can achieve, and it's time to start now.

Calendar Management

Let's move on to calendar management within the scope of events and artifacts.

Remember that the team does not need an overloaded calendar. They need time to think. So, sort out your calendars for projects before you begin. Figure 5-12 is an example of a calendar that could help Scrum Teams, if that is the framework of choice.

Aug 2024

Su	Mo	Tu	We	Th	Fr	Sa
28	29	30	31	1	2	3
4	5	6	7	8	9	10
11	12	13	14	15	16	17
18	19	20	21	22	23	24
25	26	27	28	29	30	31
1	2	3	4	5	6	7

06 Aug
• Sprint Backlog and Sprint Goals Shared

08 Aug
• Brainstorming (Estimation & Refinement)

09 Aug
  Sprint Planning Meeting
  (Sprint Backlog Refinement and DOR)

12 Aug
• Sprint Kick Off

12 Aug - 23 Aug
  Sprint (With Daily Standups)

16 Aug
• Mid Sprint Check In

22 Aug
• Sprint Review/QA Sign Off/Release Planning

23 Aug
• Sprint Closure
• Release to Production
• Sanity Test
• Retrospective

Figure 5-12. *A Sample Sprint Calendar for Scrum*

Your execution won't go wrong if your team sorts out the calendar for the project.

Values

My favorite part and the shortest. People can identify a hundred odd values for you, and you can follow them in name or in practice, but it starts with honesty to yourself.

A dishonest person can neither be motivated nor committed. Such a person can never have the courage which is needed to deliver at the right time and will lack continuous improvement. So, no matter how many values are listed down for you, remember it starts with honesty.

Be honest, identify honest people in your team, and filter the rest, for your own good.

Tying Up Values and Emotions with the Framework

It is not the values themselves that are complicated; it is the act of keeping checkpoints so that people intuitively bring out the best within each other, continuously. To give a little bit of a background, I saw extremely capable people become zombies in a company that failed to extract value from them. Even if you would wish them "Happy Birthday," they'd come up with an excuse to curse the person right next to them. This section came to my mind, only because of them. What went wrong, I thought? These folks were awesome at what they did. Now, look at them. Sad...wondering where to go. It was the value system and the combined synergy. Lifestyles are complex these days. People come from varied backgrounds. Do you even think you have a chance of solving someone's behavior at your workplace? They will recur, even if you do solve them. It is where you want to focus and how you wish to tap each other's strength, sidelining the weaknesses. Studies in human behavior, however, can help a lot and should not be underrated. Values cannot be untied from emotions and intuitive abilities of the team members to perform specific functions. In this context, it is helpful to speak of a very important model to look into your own emotions at play and even the teams'. Plutchik's Wheel of Emotions is described next.

Plutchik's Wheel of Emotions

It would be strange if we speak of values without understanding emotional literacy and awareness. I strongly believe that companies need to have counsellors. How daily work eats into their mind wellness is a problem that challenges agility – and people will only vent in front of neutral parties. The energies of a team and an organization can only be set into place if you make a conscious effort to sort out your reactions.

Read the following piece of news from a heartbreaking episode:

> *Amid a social media storm over the death of a young employee at tax consultancy major EY allegedly due to work pressure, Deloitte has formed a three-member external committee, which includes former revenue secretary Tarun Bajaj, to look into practices, policies and processes concerning employees, its South Asia CEO Romal Shetty said on Friday.*
>
> —Business Standard

Now, the question arises, does pressure have anything to do with values? Well, yes and no. Someone in a situation, such as the above, forgot to take out time to understand their working capacity, someone out here did not notice declining mental health, and there could be a lack of general awareness of what's creeping into the system slowly. In other words, feelings were not named (labelled or expressed) well within time. Labelling feelings helps to diminish reactions. Even if this particular case turns out to be a false claim or say some employees are not meant for pressure, then do we just turn our back on them? Because this is happening everywhere in the world, as we speak. Being customer centric cannot mean forgetting an employee-first culture either.

Dr. Daniel Siegel, a psychiatrist, writer, and professor who is also the founding codirector of the Mindful Awareness Research Center at UCLA, developed a technique called name it to tame it. You can use any emotion wheel as a visual aid to understand what the feeling is and how it should be handled. Labelling (in your mind) the current emotions that a team is going through and finding suitable triggers is always a good start to coach your teams to the next level of productivity.

Plutchik's wheel, a renowned psychological model, categorizes eight primary emotions into opposing pairs to label what you are going through. Psychologist Robert Plutchik developed this wheel, which as shown in the following image would show you how to label emotions during conflict resolution, daily interaction, escalations, ugly management, clients from hell, and how your team members are compromising their values in the face of emotions. As leaders, we need to help each other to understand what is stopping cultural stability. Above all, we should apply it to ourselves.

Figure 5-13 shows how the Plutchik's Wheel of Emotions helps you label your emotions. If you go to the website (mentioned in the caption), you can also change the intensity of the emotion to understand what emotions are playing on your mind, with varied intensity.

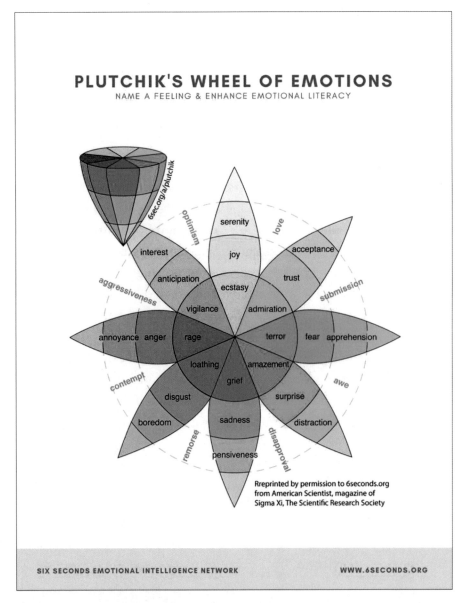

Figure 5-13. *Plutchik's Wheel of Emotions*
Source: 6seconds.org: A beautiful website for improving emotional literacy

For a long time in my career, I struggled with managers because my EQ was weak and values were strong – that's my own judgement and not of a certified authority on the subject. So, it's not values alone that will do the trick. It's your emotional control that will build the culture around you. Again, just professing all such information does not make me stand on a better platform than the reader. It's a journey, and we're all in the same boat. An in-depth study would lead you to an understanding of basic and compound emotions, but we will stick to the very basics.

How to Use the Plutchik's Wheel of Emotions

In the beginning, without getting deep into such visual aids, all you got to do is to pick words and find out how they are connected. You can, of course, use such models in depth, but relating them with one another is not only informative but also fun.

Check an emotion's place in the wheel. Emotions on the wheel increase in intensity toward the middle, and feelings are positioned as opposites because they represent contrasting physiological responses and experiences – this is not to say that they don't result from one another. The key trick however is to connect the dots. If there is a lot of **boredom**, it's perhaps people are **accepting** the present state as is, without innovation, but if it escalates negatively, it turns into **disgust**, and you might lose a potentially good candidate. If you notice such an employee, you'll engage him in something that the employee finds interesting. And the employee will give back more to the company because the mind stimulates itself in other use cases. So, you use **acceptance** partially and give them more opportunities to **trust** you for getting work that will retain them and, better still, work of their **interest** that will increase the level of **optimism**.

I worked with a manager who constantly lied about me to the senior management. It shocked me, frankly. Her dishonesty stemmed from her insecurity however. And her **fear** told me that *she thought* her job was at risk because of me, which kept her constantly in some kind of an

apprehension. Later I found out, every peer was treated the same way. Her lying was a mere consequence to protect her own position in the company. Sometimes, such reasoning can help you understand someone's position becomes clearer. It helps you decide. Either you can help yourself in the situation, or you find a threshold. Questioning each other's value systems will not help – it will only result in social media posts about toxic bosses!

Contempt is a secondary negative emotion on Plutchik's Wheel, resulting from a combination of **anger** and **disgust**. There was a manager who belittled my ideas and dismissed my work in front of large groups of people – the amount of anger and disgust that I felt those days affected me in ways that have lasted for years. Well...no guide on agility can help you change the values the manager should have had, but the moment I understood that my contempt is killing me and that all the manager wanted was **undue submission**, I walked out. What I did inadvertently was that I labelled those feelings and gauged the root cause.

Such exercises help you to find teams that match your emotional quotient to move toward joy, trust, interest, optimism, and the like. It helps you find what you seek in life – emotional stability at work.

Out of your daily work routine, if you dare to ask your team members, ask them one simple question – "How safe do you feel?" That answer should tell you whether your framework is operationally correct or not. And it should serve as an important measure for your framework. Speaking of safety, let us move toward the one thing that makes us appreciate our employers the most – the culture of the company we work for.

Organizational Culture

Everything when tied up together denotes culture. The values you stand for, the agility you carry, and the workload your employees have – everything has its place in defining culture. One of the most important factors is psychological safety.

Psychological Safety in an Organization

No framework can succeed without this much talked about concept. Psychological safety is the belief that a team environment is safe for interpersonal risk-taking. Coined by Amy Edmondson, it refers to a culture where individuals feel confident expressing their ideas, questions, concerns, and mistakes without fear of embarrassment, rejection, or punishment.

This concept is a cornerstone of high-performing teams, fostering open communication, trust, and collaboration. It enables creativity, problem-solving, and innovation, as team members feel valued and respected. Psychological safety also promotes learning and adaptability, as mistakes are viewed as opportunities for growth rather than failures.

In practice, psychological safety requires:

1. **Inclusive Leadership**: Leaders encourage participation, listen actively, and show empathy.

2. **Constructive Feedback**: Teams prioritize open, nonjudgmental discussions.

3. **Mutual Respect**: Diversity of thought is celebrated, and conflicts are handled collaboratively.

By cultivating psychological safety, organizations can enhance employee engagement, well-being, and performance, creating a resilient and thriving work culture.

You don't need intensive studies to make your teams feel safe. You need to be human enough.

I was speaking to Garima Sharma, a senior manager in the Research and Impact team, in a leading NGO in Northeast India, about the term psychological safety. Here's what she had to say.

As a manager, I feel that it's important to ensure the wellbeing of each and every team member. This begins with having an open, genuine, non-judgmental, and non-competitive space for them to share their ideas and concerns. Building good relationships is core to building good teams.

Some people keep it simple. And it is in a simple approach that you find good culture. Good organizational culture isn't built on frameworks alone – it thrives on genuine human connection. Psychological safety, at its core, is about creating spaces where people feel valued, respected, and heard. As Garima Sharma aptly put it, building strong teams starts with simple yet authentic relationships. Sometimes, the best culture comes from keeping it casual, approachable, and real.

We will now introduce two models, which serve as a good way to provide practical pathways to enhance psychological safety, enabling teams to thrive in a culture of trust, openness, and shared purpose. We are referring to the **Belbin Team Model** and **Thomas–Kilmann Conflict Mode Instrument (TKI)**. Belbin helps teams appreciate diverse strengths, fostering mutual respect and collaboration, while TKI equips teams to navigate conflicts constructively.

The Belbin Team Model

The Belbin Team Model is a framework that identifies nine distinct team roles, each with its own strengths and weaknesses. Developed by Dr. Meredith Belbin, this model helps individuals understand their natural tendencies and how they can contribute to a team's success. Throughout my life, from school to college and then a job and a failed startup – I understood that when you force fit a person into a role that doesn't match with his abilities, or his interest, he is bound to bend toward negative emotions – most likely insecurity.

So, understanding what role is meant for you or for people in your team is the most important part of resource allocation.

The Nine Belbin Team Roles

1. **Chair:** Provides leadership, direction, and decision-making. Such people make good functional leaders, coaches, and the like.

2. **Plant:** Generates creative ideas and innovative solutions. Allocate such people to product engineering, R&D, marketing, etc.

3. **Specialist:** Contributes expert knowledge and technical skills. Such people are needed for execution but maybe at a technical leadership level.

4. **Monitor Evaluator:** Analyzes and assesses information, making objective judgments.

5. **Implementer:** Turns ideas into practical actions and plans. Again, needed for execution.

6. **Team worker:** Fosters teamwork, cooperation, and harmony. Qualities you'd like in a good Scrum Master.

7. **Resource Investigator:** Explores opportunities, networks, and gathers information. An obvious choice for sales and strategy.

8. **Shaper:** Challenges the team, drives action, and overcomes obstacles. Again, a good Scrum Master and/or an agile coach.

9. **Completer Finisher:** Ensures attention to detail and deadlines are met. Qualities of a good Product Owner and/or a Scrum Master.

Using the Belbin Model

Each team member typically has a dominant role, but they may also exhibit characteristics of other roles. The key to effective teamwork is to recognize and appreciate the unique contributions of each individual.

Benefits of the Belbin Model

- **Self-awareness:** Individuals can gain a better understanding of their strengths and weaknesses.

- **Team Effectiveness:** Teams can identify gaps in their roles and work together more effectively.

- **Personal Development:** Individuals can develop their skills and take on new challenges.

- **Conflict Resolution:** The model can help identify and address potential conflicts within teams.

The Belbin Model can be used in various settings, including the following:

- **Team Building:** To assess team dynamics and identify areas for improvement.

- **Recruitment:** To select candidates who complement existing team members.

- **Leadership Development:** To help leaders understand their own role and the roles of their team members.

- **Personal Development:** To identify individual strengths and areas for growth.

How Belbin Supports Psychological Safety

Recognition of Strengths and Contributions

1. By identifying each member's **team role** (e.g., plant, coordinator, team worker), individuals feel valued for their unique contributions.

2. People are less likely to feel overlooked or misunderstood, as their role within the team is acknowledged and respected.

Minimizing Role Conflicts

1. Role clarity reduces overlaps and friction, as individuals know what is expected of them and where they add value.

2. When conflicts are role-related (e.g., two "shapers" competing for control), teams can address it constructively using Belbin insights.

Promoting Inclusivity

1. By recognizing the importance of all roles, including less visible ones (like the "monitor evaluator" or "completer-finisher"), teams develop a culture of inclusiveness where every member feels important.

Reducing Judgment and Bias

1. Understanding that different team roles naturally approach problems in diverse ways reduces judgment. For instance, a "plant" who thrives on creativity and out-of-the-box ideas won't be criticized for lacking detailed focus.

Balanced Teams Foster Trust

1. When teams are balanced (a mix of thinkers, doers, and relationship-builders), there is greater trust that the team can tackle challenges effectively. This trust forms a key part of psychological safety.

We were once working on a winery management system, and I had a team of ten. We followed Scrum, and from what we experienced, our synergy was good – without any friction and a complete understanding of another. The same people, with other managers, were branded negatively or even ostracized. Reason? Their core competencies were not recognized as such, when working with other managers. They were judged for the work they were given, not the work they were good at. I remember one such kid who was a very good functional leader, but many judged him for his work in the specialist domain. The result was a lot of blame game – for nothing. Again, it's like putting an automation tester in manual testing – you are confusing two specializations. An automation tester needs to work on test cases and then automation logic and reruns and analysis. A manual tester will look through the app with his eye for detail. The mindset is different. I've seen a senior tester pushing so hard to do manual testing that for a year I was baffled by his lack of performance – much later in the cycle, I realized he was working on something that he was not cut out for. He automated a system for us and cut the cost by 60 hours a month for testing, for 10 months. That amounts to 600 hours worth saving. Telling you, your weakest link might be strong in an area you did not realize. Before I conclude the chapter, let us speak of the **Thomas–Kilmann Conflict Mode Instrument (TKI)**, a tool used to assess individuals' preferred conflict-handling styles. It provides insight into how people approach and manage conflict in interpersonal or group settings, helping teams navigate disagreements effectively.

The Thomas–Kilmann Conflict Mode Instrument

Conflict resolution is crucial for fostering a healthy organizational culture, as unresolved disputes can lead to misunderstandings, decreased morale, and reduced productivity. Effective conflict resolution ensures that disagreements are addressed constructively, promoting open communication, mutual respect, and collaboration.

In one of my previous organizations, which happened to be a startup, I escalated matters of dishonesty and politics to the founder – who, by the way, was honest. The tricky part was that he didn't see dishonesty as a threat. There was constant conflict between me and a reporting manager because of her lies, and the founder just gave a flat reply, "Kanika, I am not stepping between the two of you." It was then when I realized that if conflicts are not handled, well in time they can lead to bad vibes and even long-standing disputes. A culture that prioritizes conflict resolution demonstrates a commitment to fairness and inclusivity.

The TKI model identifies five conflict-handling styles (discussed next), each varying along two dimensions:

1. **Assertiveness**: The extent to which a person tries to satisfy their own concerns.

2. **Cooperativeness**: The extent to which a person tries to satisfy others' concerns.

Overview of TKI

The five styles identified in the model are as follows:

1. **Competing (High Assertiveness, Low Cooperativeness):** A power-oriented approach where an individual prioritizes their own concerns over others.

2. **Collaborating (High Assertiveness, High Cooperativeness):** Seeking solutions that satisfy everyone's concerns; win-win.

3. **Compromising (Moderate Assertiveness, Moderate Cooperativeness):** Finding a middle ground where both parties give up something.

4. **Avoiding (Low Assertiveness, Low Cooperativeness):** Dodging conflict altogether or delaying resolution.

5. **Accommodating (Low Assertiveness, High Cooperativeness):** Prioritizing others' concerns over one's own.

The case I cited in the beginning of the section was avoiding conflict; while many leaders do that to save time, many psychologists state this as a primary cause for stress in an employee's life. What could have helped me was the founder's **assertiveness** where work ethic and morals were at stake and **compromising** where he found that both parties were right in their own position. If this is not the work of a founder, then it should be given to an HR team.

When you conduct your retrospectives, it is helpful to understand whether such aspects of team work are being addressed and, if not, then how can they be. We are all learning, and without stating the model, without making it sound deep and intelligent, we can take a step forward toward a more human-centric culture.

The Founder's Agility

As the driving force behind vision, values, and decision-making, the founder's ability to adapt, respond to challenges, and model desired behaviors directly impacts the culture of the organization.

A founder's agility is reflected in their capacity to pivot, when necessary, embrace feedback, and evolve with the needs of the team and the market. Founders pick the core team, and they decide how fast and how slow the organization will grow and what that growth may cost them. It is their mind that is reflected in the culture of the company, because the core team further expands with their vision in mind.

Leadership Styles

Understanding leadership styles is essential for fostering effective communication, collaboration, and organizational success. Extensive research has been done on the topic, and covering examples from all styles is not possible in one book. However, the reader is encouraged to notice the shift in his own leadership styles, with changing situations, and make conscious steps to increase self-awareness.

Autocratic Leadership

- **Description:** Leaders make decisions unilaterally, expecting people to follow instructions without input.

- **Advantages:** Efficient decision-making and clear direction, especially when team members need a direction coming from the leader himself.

- **Disadvantages:** Can lead to low morale, lack of creativity, disrespect, and weakly bonded teams.

Democratic Leadership

- **Description:** Leaders involve team members in decision-making processes, valuing their input.

- **Advantages:** Encourages collaboration and boosts morale.

- **Disadvantages:** Decision-making can be slower.

Laissez-Faire Leadership

- **Description:** Leaders provide minimal direction, allowing team members to make decisions.

- **Advantages:** Promotes autonomy and fosters innovation.

- **Disadvantages:** Can result in the lack of direction and accountability issues.

Transformational Leadership

- **Description:** Leaders inspire and motivate teams to exceed expectations through a shared vision.

- **Advantages:** Drives innovation and enhances engagement.

- **Disadvantages:** May overlook details and can be overly idealistic.

Transactional Leadership

- **Description:** Leaders focus on routine and structure.

- **Advantages:** Clear expectations and effective in environments where people are good with defined roles and do not wish to overstep.

- **Disadvantages:** Limited creativity and can lead to low morale. For example, this will not work with Scrum, because everybody is an equal stakeholder in Scrum.

Servant Leadership

- **Description:** Leaders prioritize the needs of their team, focusing on their development and well-being.
- **Advantages:** Builds trust and enhances collaboration.
- **Disadvantages:** May be perceived as lacking authority.

Bureaucratic Leadership

- **Description:** Leaders adhere strictly to rules and procedures.
- **Advantages:** Ensures consistency and reduces errors.
- **Disadvantages:** Can stifle innovation and lead to rigidity.

Charismatic Leadership

- **Description:** Leaders inspire enthusiasm and loyalty through their personal charm and energy.
- **Advantages:** Motivates and energizes teams.
- **Disadvantages:** Dependence on the leader and potential for manipulation.

Coaching Leadership

- **Description:** Leaders focus on developing individuals' skills and potential.
- **Advantages:** Promotes personal growth and enhances performance.
- **Disadvantages:** Time-consuming and requires significant effort.

Pacesetting Leadership

- **Description:** Leaders set high performance standards and lead by example.

- **Advantages:** Drives high performance and sets clear expectations.

- **Disadvantages:** Can overwhelm team members and may lead to burnout.

Visionary Leadership

- **Description:** Leaders articulate a clear and compelling vision for the future.

- **Advantages:** Inspires and aligns teams toward common goals.

- **Disadvantages:** May lack attention to detail and can be unrealistic.

Affiliative Leadership

- **Description:** Leaders prioritize creating harmony and emotional bonds within the team.

- **Advantages:** Enhances team cohesion and boosts morale.

- **Disadvantages:** May avoid necessary confrontations and can lead to complacency.

Situational Leadership

- **Description:** Leaders adjust their style based on the maturity and competence of their team members.

- **Advantages:** Flexible and responsive to team needs.

- **Disadvantages:** Requires high self-awareness and can be inconsistent.

Participative Leadership

- **Description:** Leaders involve team members in decision-making processes.

- **Advantages:** Encourages collaboration and increases commitment.

- **Disadvantages:** Decision-making can be slower and may lead to conflicts.

Democratic Leadership

- **Description:** Leaders make decisions based on the input of each team member.

- **Advantages:** Promotes team engagement and fosters creativity.

- **Disadvantages:** Can be time-consuming and may lead to indecision.

From a personal viewpoint, nobody can be branded into one leadership style. Talk to different people on different occasions about the same leader, and they will give you a different opinion. Why? Because there is a situational leader in all of us. The more conscious that leader is, the more chances of him understanding the situation he is facing. Again, we as authors can just show the direction and leave the reader to continue exploring such topics.

A Note on All Those Subtle Things We Never Value

You'd find it impossible to believe, but the leaders you elect for your nation have an impact on the kind of leadership you have in office! If the leadership at a national level opposes dissent, you'll see the same behavior reflected by your managers. At a subtle level, people get to know that the biggest, powerful people are getting away with it. Every other person will begin to see success as power in hand and not as strength and courage. As of writing this book, this is a sad reality in India. Like many countries of the world, leadership challenges are coming to the fore, and that is because people elected these leaders. There is representation for such silent dictatorship. Will that not show in office culture? We shall leave it to the reader to ponder on the matter.

Summary

This chapter served as a crucial stepping stone toward building effective agile frameworks. It lays the groundwork by highlighting the key elements to consider and a human-centric approach for breaking down what could become your chosen approach toward execution. We explored how these elements come together and make organizational culture while introducing you to understand your teams. All this information can help agile coaches and leaders in the industry, for practical application. In the next chapter, we look at the buzz around AI and agility, a solution that Basecamp has arrived at as an alternative to Scrum, and how to make a framework of our own.

Further Reading

- **Team Topologies**: Organizing Business and Technology Teams for Fast Flow by Manuel Pais and Matthew Skelton (2019)

- Conway's Law **by Melvin Conway (1968)**

Exercise

1. Observe your team according to the Belbin Model, and wherever your team members face a conflict, try out the Thomas–Kilmann model.

2. Inspect the framework you follow at your place of work, and see if the elements of the framework are working in collaboration. Look into artifacts, actors, events, and value systems – and then try and understand where problems are stemming from, if at all.

3. Once you identify problems in a scenario at a workplace, given the elements we discussed in this chapter, work toward a solution.

CHAPTER 6

Crafting Your Own Agile Framework

Neither the book nor this chapter intends to make a framework that will help in all your projects. We can't step into your shoes and identify your problems for you, but we can orient you and give you examples. The best thing about this chapter is that it's short and sweet. It gives an example framework that we built for a product I was working on, which worked for us. We don't wish to deep dive into our approach – the author and the team has already done their bit in the preceding chapters to reflect on the approach you are using and see what works for you. This chapter just puts into practice what has already been discussed before. Before deciding on your approach, ask yourself – why a custom approach? Why not tried and tested frameworks? Well, shaping a product through those very frameworks will inevitably make you come face to face with a problem that has not been defined. Nobody can replace personal experience, and so nobody can step into your shoes and make an approach work for you. That's where the idea of a custom approach comes from. I begin by speaking of problems that I faced in Scrum and the solution that I thought of at a framework level.

© Kanika Sud 2025
K. Sud, *Customizable Agile Development*, https://doi.org/10.1007/979-8-8688-1055-8_6

Problems with Scrum

During the implementation of Scrum, one can fairly question what the downsides of the framework are. Since it is purposefully abstract, does it leave loose ends that need to be tied? Is tweaking a bad idea? What are the inherent problems? Let's speak of the most common problems that I encountered during my experience.

Lack of Specific Skill Set for Scrum Masters

Scrum does not explicitly address the necessary skill set for a Scrum Master, leading to the common issue of hiring individuals who may lack deep technical understanding. Scrum Masters who are unfamiliar with engineering processes or the intricacies of development work can struggle to facilitate Scrum effectively. As per the **Scrum Guide**:

> *The Scrum Master is accountable for establishing Scrum as defined in the Scrum Guide. They do this by helping everyone understand Scrum theory and practice, both within the Scrum Team and the organization.*

While this highlights the Scrum Master's role in promoting Scrum principles, it doesn't emphasize the need for technical knowledge or expertise. A Scrum Master without a clear understanding of the engineering challenges faced by the team may be less effective in resolving impediments or guiding technical improvements.

Unclear Guidance on Writing Product Backlog Items

Another common challenge is the lack of clear direction on how to write effective Product Backlog Items (PBIs). While the Scrum framework is intentionally high-level and adaptable, having practical guidelines would be immensely helpful, especially when it comes to **vertical vs. horizontal slicing** of backlog items. This can be a challenge for teams looking to break

188

down work into manageable chunks that can deliver value incrementally. The **INVEST** principle, if pointed out within the framework guide itself, can help people adopt the framework better.

The Emergence of Agile Coaches Despite Scrum Masters

The role of an **Agile Coach** has emerged in many organizations, even where Scrum Masters are present. This raises an important question: Why has this role gained prominence despite Scrum Masters being accountable for coaching the team on Agile practices?

- Was the **Scrum Master role insufficiently defined**, or were their responsibilities too focused on Scrum processes rather than broader Agile principles?

- Did organizations feel the need for Agile Coaches to fill gaps in skills or expertise that Scrum Masters were unable to address?

The rise of Agile Coaches suggests that many teams or organizations may not have fully equipped Scrum Masters with the necessary *agility* or *skill set* to handle team dynamics, organizational alignment, or the nuances of Agile transformations.

Scrum Lays No Emphasis on Agile Contracts

The role of an agile contract is glaringly ignored in Scrum. What if you have a contract to design a mobile application for three months. After three months, the contract was renewed and the designs are handed over to developers, and they find out that some items cannot be developed. What went wrong here? The contract was not agile enough. It kept no room for changing prototypes during the development contract. Even though Scrum is about implementation, there has to be a hint for how the contract should be drawn in such cases.

If you wish to catch up on contracting for Agile, a good report from KPMG is given in the section for further reading.

Scrum for Software

Scrum is designed to be universally applicable across industries; its guidelines do not directly address critical practices in the software industry, such as **Continuous Integration (CI)** and **Continuous Delivery (CD)**. For teams working in software development, a framework that incorporates these practices is essential for ensuring efficient, automated delivery pipelines. Given that Scrum is widely used in software development, it would be beneficial to supplement the Scrum Guide with an understanding of CI/CD practices that align with Agile principles.

The video "Continuous Integration vs Feature Branch Workflow" (follow the link, to watch the full video) discusses two prevalent development workflows: Continuous Integration (CI) and Feature Branching, advocating the former. Remember, the key:

> *the fundamental assumption of CI is that there's only one interesting version, the current one.*

> —C2Wiki

In the **Continuous Integration** approach, developers frequently commit directly to the main branch, ensuring that integrations occur continuously. This method emphasizes immediate feedback, rapid detection of integration issues, and maintaining a consistently deployable codebase. However, it requires a high level of team discipline to prevent broken builds from affecting the entire team.

Conversely, the **Feature Branching** workflow involves developers creating separate branches for individual features or tasks. These branches are merged into the main branch upon completion, often through pull requests. This strategy allows for isolated development and thorough code reviews but can lead to challenges such as merge conflicts and delayed integration, potentially causing integration issues to surface later in the development process.

The video suggests that while both workflows are widely used, they are mutually exclusive, and teams should carefully consider their specific needs and capabilities when choosing between them.

Scrum Takes a One-Size-Fits-All Approach

I often wondered why Scrum was so straightforward to define yet so challenging to master. When I became an Agile Coach, the reasons became clear. Many teams adopting Scrum were not evaluated for their agile maturity before diving into the framework. Similarly, Scrum Masters were seldom assessed for their understanding of agility, leaving gaps in their ability to guide teams effectively. This lack of assessment often led to misaligned expectations and hindered the successful adoption of Scrum practices.

All these problems led me to think of Scrum++.

Scrum++

In Scrum++, I address the problems I mentioned above. I haven't detailed estimation, because like everything in agile, estimation is practice. And story points are a good way to understand if your teams are delivering whatever they are committing.

Again, this framework does not challenge years of Scrum being in practice; it is out of personal experience with Scrum.

By introducing refined roles, events, values, and guidance, Scrum++ aims to bridge the gaps observed in traditional Scrum practices. It retains the foundational principles of Scrum while extending its application to tackle common implementation challenges. First, let's elaborate the agile maturity assessment step.

Agile Maturity in Scrum++

Before adopting Scrum++, we assess team and organizational maturity:

1. **Team Agility**

    - Evaluate understanding and application of Agile principles at a team and organization level.

2. **Scrum Technical Lead Readiness**

    - Assess technical and coaching skills, along with the understanding of Scrum and Agile.

3. **Contractual Flexibility**

    - Review current contract structures for adaptability.

The author advises not to go into the intricacies of maturity models but to consult an Agile Coach and know where you stand and why you're there. To see how you could go ahead in the path of agility from there onward. In general, if the entire team has a Scrum Certification and has an understanding of the reasons behind the Agile Manifesto. Developers need to have a Scrum Certified Developer cert, and Scrum Masters need to have a Scrum Master cert. Same for the Product Owner. Every single person needs to be certified *and have an understanding of why Scrum is needed, as a philosophy*. Notice the emphasis on philosophy and need. There are many empty Scrum certification holders lying out there and little who appreciate agile and Scrum.

It is because of the agile maturity assessment as a prestep, we include a recommended but optional role of an agile coach in the team. Let us now describe the actors.

Actors

Keep in mind everything we learnt about actors in the previous chapter and, if necessary, take notes on how you want your accountabilities to be. With that said, you should also focus on the problems faced for accountability in Scrum.

Scrum Technical Lead

This is an evolved role that emphasizes both technical and coaching expertise. A key aspect of this role is that it highlights a strong technical foundation while retaining the Scrum identity. Here, by technical, we don't mean software tech – anybody who knows the implementation details or the technicality of the project, including various components, and has the right technical experience and aptitude can lead the product. This person *must* pass the Agility assessment of the team (mentioned in the previous section), according to the scoring level of the Agile Coach (described later in this section). In the absence of an external Agile Coach, the senior most Scrum Master should be assessing the Scrum technical lead. Due to people factors, it is best to appoint an agile coach, external to the team and the organization, whose task is not to involve himself with projects but just to assess, coach, and repeat. More on that when the last actor is described in this section.

Accountabilities:

- Ensuring the team adheres to both Scrum principles and engineering best practices.

- Possessing foundational technical knowledge to guide teams effectively in resolving impediments.

- Coaching the team on Agile principles beyond Scrum-specific practices.

- Ensuring Sprints are delivered on time and if not having a technical justification for the same.

- Being accountable for the technical health of a product, at any given time – even though the responsibility is of the entire team.

- Decide a team topology that works for his team according to expectations of the client.

Skill Set:

- A mandatory understanding of Scrum through certifications *and* assessment by the Agile Coach or Senior Scrum Master.

- Experience in delivering cross-functional solutions in engineering, as required by the team. The Scrum Master should have all the skill sets of the individual team members.

- To assess resources in the team who are not able to perform, the Scrum technical lead needs to be adept with resource assessment, resource identification, and resource allocation. This is in accordance with the clause on Technical Excellence in the Agile Manifesto.

Agile Product Strategist

The Agile Product Strategist focuses on improved backlog management and defining acceptance criteria for all user stories.

Accountabilities:

- Writing user stories using the **INVEST principle**.

- Ensuring clear **vertical slicing** of backlog items for incremental value delivery.

- Collaborating with the Scrum Technical Lead to ensure alignment with engineering constraints.

- Collaborating with the Team, spearheading the Sprint backlog efforts, and marking complexity on all items based on story point estimation.

- Understanding the team's empirical capacity to deliver features and stories. For example, if the team can deliver one feature, vertically sliced into epics and stories in one Sprint, it becomes the responsibility of the Scrum *Technical Lead and the Agile Product Strategist* to clearly call out any work overload.

- To call out any nonagile contract that affects the health of the product.

- To be able to present a percentage health of the product in terms of bugs, code quality, and team performance to the project sponsors and all Scrum stakeholders.

- Taking a sign off from all the Scrum Team members about the definition of ready, before they start executing a user story.

Skill Set:

- Clear understanding of vertical slicing

- Clear understanding of the INVEST principle

- Good backlog management ability

- Understanding velocity, lead time, etc. as Agile Metrics

Agile Coach (Optional)

This role, seen as unnecessary by many, is a good addition, especially considering the value that a good agile coach can add.

Accountabilities:

- Bringing agile as a social change. Encouraging people to be agile, rather than following agile

- Assessing the team's agility and maturity on agile as well as Scrum methods

- Assessing the Scrum technical lead's agility and maturity on Scrum methods

- To introduce the Agile Manifesto, it's principles, and values on an organizational level

- To regularly conduct meetings with Scrum Team Leads to understand their pain points and coach them on Scrum and Agile

- To make sure that Agility is adopted on a more human-centric level

- To make sure that the company's culture and the team's culture align with agility

- Addressing systemic issues that may fall outside the Scrum Team's purview

- To understand conflict management in teams and assist individual Scrum Masters while at the same time observing their way of establishing peaceful, productive teams

- Organizing workshops for people to speak of process, people, methods, and execution-first problems

- To encourage Agile Contracts at a company level

Guidance on Agile Contracts

Scrum++ emphasizes the importance of Agile Contracts:

- **Collaborative Flexibility**

  - Contracts must allow iterative feedback and adjustment of deliverables.

- **Shared Risk and Reward**

  - Encourages mechanisms like milestone-based payments tied to reviewed and accepted Increments.

- **Development-Ready Design**

  - Contracts for design or discovery phases must explicitly include provisions for adaptability during development.

Like we said before, Agile Coaches have emerged, because Scrum Masters are busy executing projects and establishing Scrum in teams. They need an observer too.

Skill Set:

- Certified Agile Coach

- Clear understanding of Scrum

- Good to have knowledge of human behavioral and cultural assessment models

Scrum++ Team

This is similar to the Scrum Team in the fact that it is cross-functional and the accountabilities are also retained from the original Scrum Guide. The only topping we wish to add is the Team Topology.

We leave it to the Scrum Technical Lead to decide a team topology that works for his team, but deciding on one for a project is a key accountability for him.

Events

Apart from the regular Scrum events (Sprint, Daily Scrum Meet, Sprint Planning, Sprint Review, Sprint Retrospective), we introduce the following **mandatory** events:

1. **Backlog Grooming (Which Was Optional in Scrum)**: It should be done regularly, as the team decides, but should never be missed. Adding acceptance criteria, with the help of the team's questions on the user stories, is the primary objective of the event. Prioritization, discussing risks associated with items, and impact analysis – everything about the backlog, which is not covered in the regular Scrum events, is done here. You are to make the backlog better. How you do it is an art, and it comes with practice.

   You can take the help of our Calendar Management section in Chapter 5, on how to organize such events.

2. **CI/CD Review:** A 15-min check on how you are deploying your work and if that makes sense with industry best practices. Continuous Integration vs. Feature Branching was discussed earlier, and you should understand more such best practices during this event. If we don't declare this as a mandate, it gets ignored.

A few recommended practices:

Continuous Integration might only apply to software, but how you mark a feature deployed, applies to every line of work.

Values

The Scrum++ framework retains the Scrum values (Commitment, Courage, Focus, Openness, and Respect) while introducing:

1. **Adaptability**: Emphasizing the ability to pivot based on changes in the environment, team dynamics, or requirements

2. **Honesty**: Emphasizing on honesty to self and to others

3. **Vision**: Emphasizing on the team member's vision for the team and for the self

Summary

We tried addressing the problems in Scrum, based on personal experience, making best practices a mandate of the framework itself. We also highlighted the importance of Agile Coaches and Agile Contracts. I'd say that don't let the world overrate the word agile to the extent that you get caught in processes that you don't fully understand. Focus on philosophy, be understanding enough, and use common sense as a driver to figure out the best approach for yourselves. But remember that agile and agility can never die. Be agile, don't just follow agile! If you've come thus far, you still relate with whatever I have presented in the book, and you know now, that if someone professes that people do not need a book to be agile, well, the world needed a manifesto to wake up. It's good to remind yourself, once a while!

Further Reading

Contracting for Agile – A Report By KPMG

CHAPTER 7

Keeping It All Human Centric

We've spoken about empathy, collaboration, and the like when appropriate. They are certainly understood principles, but the main point I wish to raise here is much simpler but more profound: we are human beings. Expecting ourselves and others to function in a rigid, machine like manner is, frankly, inhuman. This is why a human-centric focus is crucial when understanding and applying Agile. Therefore, it's important to remind ourselves of not looking outward for a concept called "agility" but tapping the best within us. It's that simple.

Why the Talk Around Human Centricity

Agile is a way of thinking, living, and interacting that reflects human qualities such as adaptability, resilience, and creativity. We have long professed the idea of introducing Agile as a form of social change – something that extends beyond the confines of the workplace and integrates into daily life. In this context, it is fitting to explore who has demonstrated agility throughout history. These individuals were not just agile in their careers but in their thinking and actions, continuously adapting, learning, and evolving.

© Kanika Sud 2025
K. Sud, *Customizable Agile Development*, https://doi.org/10.1007/979-8-8688-1055-8_7

By looking at historical figures who embodied these principles – whether through intellectual growth, social change, or personal transformation – we can find examples where agility was not just a concept but a lived experience. Let's take a look.

Agility Throughout History

I want to talk about ancient civilizations and even nomadic behaviour. What was human kind doing then? It was continuously learning, adapting, thinking critically. We cannot help ourselves doing such things, can we, now? Then, why should we treat this as an external concept? Why aren't we mapping it to who we already are?

Ancient Greeks showed intellectual agility and their willingness to challenge the status quo. Especially Socrates. Socrates was known for the critical dialogue he encouraged and the way he challenged assumptions. Socrates prioritized interactive dialogue at a time when instruction was thought to be the right way to teach. He encouraged self-awareness. There is this famous anecdote where Socrates, in a display of remarkable intellectual humility, acknowledged that his wisdom lay in his awareness of his own ignorance, stating "I am wiser than this man, for neither of us appears to know anything great and good; but he fancies he knows something, although he knows nothing; whereas I, as I do not know anything, so I do not fancy I do..." – a sentiment that epitomizes the agile mindset. It is the agile mindset that encourages us to look within – with retrospective being one such tool – to identify our own knowledge gaps, rather than assume we have all the answers. Sparking collective learning, just like we do in daily Scrums, and embracing continuous learning, which is mentioned in the agile manifesto and prioritizing critical thinking, were all introduced in the Socratic method, long before the formalization of modern agile practices and methodologies emerged.

Talk about hunter-gatherers, in our ancestors. Their way of surviving was to adapt to change. They didn't need to sign a manifesto for it. You can laugh at this line today, but if it comes from a scientist, you'll only be forced to think inward.

Let us see a few more examples and map them to agility. Take empiricism, for instance. The name John Locke comes to mind. There is historical evidence to state how Locke experienced diverse environments and admitted learning through such exposure. For instance, during his political exile in Holland (1683–1689), he interacted with a variety of thinkers and ideas, including Protestant reformers, skeptics, and scientists. This exposure affirmed his belief in the empirical foundations of knowledge, as he observed how diverse experiences and environments shaped individuals' beliefs. Locke reflected on how humans develop ideas from infancy to adulthood. He noted that babies seem to lack any complex ideas or knowledge at birth and instead gradually acquire understanding through sensory experiences and personal reflections. He posited that the mind starts as a blank slate (tabula rasa) and that experience "writes" on it, forming all knowledge over time. The idea behind mentioning this here is that many people throughout the world have recognized the same pillars on which frameworks like Scrum stand.

Galileo Galilei's confrontation with the Church stands as a defining moment in scientific history. In 1610, using his improved telescope, he observed moons orbiting Jupiter, providing strong evidence for the Copernican model of a Sun-centered universe. When he published these findings, he faced fierce opposition from the Catholic Church, which held to the geocentric view. Despite being tried for heresy and placed under house arrest, Galileo continued his work, demonstrating resilience and a commitment to empirical truth. His ability to adapt to constraints and focus on incremental progress reflects an unwavering pursuit of better solutions despite obstacles. Scientists for that matter operate on continuous improvement, for nothing else will help them discover.

Gargi Vachaknavi, during a philosophical debate at King Janaka's court, fearlessly questioned Sage Yajnavalkya about the essence of existence. She asked profound questions about the nature of reality and the underlying principle that sustains the universe. When Yajnavalkya acknowledged her intellectual depth, Gargi cemented her place as one of the earliest proponents of fearless inquiry in Indian philosophy. Her emphasis on open dialogue and iterative questioning shows the power of collaboration in refining understanding and reaching clarity. It was her way of achieving excellence, which enhances agility.

Aristotle's study of biology demonstrates his empirical approach. He spent years observing animals and plants, meticulously recording their anatomy and behaviour. His observations laid the groundwork for future biological sciences, showing his respect for metrics and his commitment to building knowledge from direct experience. His method highlights the importance of using data and observation to refine and validate hypotheses over time.

Alan Turing's work at Bletchley Park during World War II was marked by iterative problem-solving. Tasked with cracking the German Enigma code, Turing developed the Bombe machine, a precursor to modern computers. His methodical refinement of this technology played a crucial role in shortening the war and saving countless lives. Some historians estimate that Turing's work shortened the war in Europe by two to four years. His approach reflects the power of critical thinking and testing to solve complex problems efficiently.

Swami Vivekananda's address at the 1893 Parliament of the World's Religions in Chicago showcased his ability to adapt and inspire. Speaking to a Western audience, he articulated Indian spirituality in a way that was accessible and transformative, emphasizing the unity of all religions. His speech marked a turning point in global perceptions of Indian philosophy. This ability to tailor his message to meet the needs of diverse stakeholders exemplifies a deep understanding of user-centric communication.

Rabindranath Tagore's creation of Visva-Bharati University reflects his commitment to collaborative learning. Dissatisfied with rote education, he established a space where students could engage with nature, arts, and global cultures. His approach blended traditional Indian values with modern educational ideals, fostering creativity and innovation. This willingness to experiment with and refine educational practices demonstrates a mindset oriented toward sustainable and impactful change.

Sri Aurobindo's transformation from a revolutionary to a spiritual leader is a story of introspection. After being imprisoned for his role in India's independence struggle, he experienced a profound spiritual awakening. This inner journey led him to develop an integrative philosophy that combined personal and collective progress, inspiring leaders and thinkers worldwide. His journey underscores the value of seeking feedback and aligning internal goals with broader missions to drive meaningful transformation.

Swami Vivekananda spoke of continuous improvement by introducing the east to the west, in a manner that both civilizations could understand each other. His step, coming at a time of political tumult, was filled with openness and courage. He was ready to adapt to global exposure. The key principles were still the same, even though he wasn't delivering a project!

Dig deep into the thought process of progressive thinkers, and you'll find that they responded to change, worked in shorter learning cycles, respected metrics, worked collaboratively, sought within, enabled leaders, paid attention to excellence, and more. All of these are nothing but paraphrased principles of Agile.

Pause a bit, and think of why human beings learn continuously? Why don't we just stop learning? Why can't we stop thinking? Let's see in the next section.

The Cellular Science of Agility

We asked you why human beings can't help adapting. It's how human cells are. Human cells' adaptability can be compared to organizational systems emphasizing the parallels between biological systems and organizational structures. Human cells, much like elements in an organization, function independently yet interdependently, responding to external stimuli to ensure the survival and efficiency of the whole. In this context, each cell has a specialized role, analogous to employees or departments within an organization, contributing to the overall function. When cells adapt to changing environments—whether by replicating, altering functions, or reorganizing—it mirrors how organizations shift in response to market dynamics or internal challenges.

The theory of complex adaptive systems (CAS) explains this relationship further. CAS refers to systems made up of diverse, interacting components that adapt to their environment, evolving over time without central control. We explained that bit in Chapter 5. These systems are characterized by self-organization, interdependence, and a capacity for learning, much like an organization adjusting to new information, competition, or societal needs. The adaptability of both cells and organizations is a key feature of CAS; they react and evolve based on feedback loops, reshaping to maintain function in a changing environment.

In leadership and management theory, complex adaptive leadership emphasizes an approach where multiple viewpoints are embraced, and leadership responds dynamically to evolving circumstances, much like the way cells in a body adapt. Organizations that adopt this approach can better tackle "wicked problems" – complex, persistent challenges – by continuously learning, evolving, and applying new knowledge. This highlights how both biological systems and organizations thrive through adaptability, interconnection, and constant evolution, making them resilient in complex and unpredictable environments.

The Human Body

Take the example of the human body – a complex adaptive system. Reality is complex, because human behaviour governs it. Behaviour comes from the mind, and that is, after all, part of the body. You cannot isolate your behaviour at your workplace, as if human science were nothing at all.

The human body is constantly **adapting** to its environment, responding to changes in temperature, diet, exercise, and more. If we dig deeper, we realize that both positively and negatively speaking, we can map the human cell adaptivity to agile teams and agile organization. That will make it truly human centric, and the focus will be within. Take, for instance, a healthy cell – scientists will confirm that a healthy cell has clarity of its purpose, it **collaborates** effectively with other cells, it responds to changes, it learns and improves continuously, and it self-organizes. The cell isn't a hermit. It constantly collaborates with its neighbors. Through intricate signaling pathways, they share information, coordinate activities, and maintain a healthy tissue. Cells can modify gene expression patterns **based on environmental cues or past experiences**. These changes can be passed on to daughter cells during cell division, allowing for a form of "memory" and adaptation across generations of cells. That's very close to empiricism.

In contrast, take a look at cancer cells. These mutated cells grow uncontrollably. They don't collaborate, they don't respond to signals, and they are simply driven by their own agenda, prioritizing their own growth over the wellbeing of the host organism. A cancer cell masks itself to manipulate its environment. It's the antithesis of fostering **transparency** – a key agile principle. Cellular learning stops with this very selfishness. In fact, if organizations keep an eye out for such nonagile employees, they can persist their core culture which has chances of degradation over time. Furthermore, scientists say that understanding the transformation of healthy cells to mutated cells may help us form healthier societies. For instance, the diet that the cell gets not only in the form of food but also in the form of social interaction and critical thinking is imperative to how cells transform. Is that not the way societies transform as well? And just like receptors on the cellular surface mask cancerous behaviour, good, agile leaders will focus on the core behaviour and bring out the best within all individuals, not getting fooled by the manipulation of such elements in a team.

While we are still talking of leadership, let us remind ourselves that the most well-remembered leaders have been inclusive and have been honest to themselves. Fear, curbing dissent, lack of retrospect, putting an individual above the country, etc., is ultimately a lack of agility and honesty (this, by the way, was the main value I pointed out in Chapter 5), whereas jobs and duties when performed with agility and introspection lead to self-realization and breaking norms to focus on progress.

Agility in Animals

And all, this is not just true for human beings. Ever heard of the Mexican cavefish, also known as the blind cavefish (*Astyanax mexicanus*)? They are a fascinating example of convergent evolution, where a species adapts to a new environment in similar ways even though populations are isolated from each other. These fish live in a complex of caves in northeastern Mexico, with some populations having been separated from surface-dwelling relatives for millions of years. In complete darkness, sight is unnecessary, and unsurprisingly, the Mexican cavefish have lost their eyes or have eyes that are greatly reduced in size. They also lack pigment, making them appear translucent or pink. However, the Mexican cavefish have developed other adaptations to thrive in their dark environment. Their other senses are heightened, especially their sense of touch and hearing. They have long barbels around their mouths that help them navigate and find food. They can also detect faint vibrations in the water. Perhaps even more interesting is that some cavefish populations retain a rudimentary eye and can still perceive light. This leftover sensitivity may allow them to respond to changes in day and night, which can influence their biological processes even in the absence of sight. Moreover, this evolution happened both as a result of collective awareness of surroundings and time. Both being equally important. Rings a bell?

Becoming the Best Version of Yourself

Remember that it takes no heroic effort to become who you already are. You have just got to admit it and then constantly improve to become the best version of yourself. Neither should the project need heroic effort nor does your attitude change require heroism. It can be in minimal quantities, and

> *No Heroics. If you need a hero to get things done, you have a problem. Heroic effort should be viewed as a failure of planning.*
>
> —Jeff Sutherland, *Scrum: The Art of Doing Twice the Work in Half the Time*

If you can silently change one person for the better, *along with yourself,* you're on the track of making better societies. Remaining rigid and going back to ways which are not fruitful will only stop you. At the time of writing this, many countries are going through a very weird patch, where leaders are speaking of irrelevant things and twisting history and news for their own good. This is similar to any anarchy in the world, where the real focus gets distorted and what is left is a useless conversation that brings no good to anyone. And why is that, because during such a fake leadership, leaders do not move forward. They do not learn. They do not think critically; they do not adapt. They become insecure and think of themselves, and their motivation is not about the product (the society or the complex adaptive system in question); it is about retaining power. I won't even begin to speak of the havoc it's causing. I spoke earlier of current leadership challenges in many nations, and I'd leave it at that.

Now, let's get right into good news about agile adoption at an organization level.

Notes on State of Agile Report 2023

If you are an agile enthusiast, you should definitely read the State of Agile Reports. If you are not an agile enthusiast, you'll likely be experiencing a lot of tension in your workplace without going wrong. The key is the mindset and the positivity it brings with you. The key is the change at the cellular level we just spoke of. And going by quantifiable data is what will make you take that first step toward agile enthusiasm. So, let's take a look at some facts.

You can get your copy of The State of Agile Report 2023 here. While the report gives you extensive views from the world on many topics, we would like to focus on topics that concern the theme of our book.

The data was formed out of **788 survey respondents** about their perception of Agile. Citing some key takeaways with source pages:

- Agile remains essential, with 71% confirming its use in their software development life cycle (SDLC) (p. 4).

- Engineering, R&D, and product teams reported the highest growth in Agile adoption, increasing by 16% compared to last year, now at 48% of respondents.

Now, while 70% and plus is a good number, one would wonder, what others think. What might be the challenges that people are facing.

1. **Thirty-six percent** (around 284 respondents) reported that leadership resistance is a key obstacle to Agile adoption, while **47%** (around 370 respondents) cited **cultural clashes** as another significant barrier (p. 15, p. 16).

2. **Forty-six percent** of respondents (about 362 people) noted that legacy systems requiring hybrid approaches are preventing Agile from scaling (p. 17).

The first challenge I listed above is even more insightful, since many people would agree that leaders can improve culture. These are corelated, but it was important to cite these options separately, because many people see culture coming from leaders alone. Is that true? By now, it would be safe to leave that answer to the reader himself.

Legacy systems is an entirely different debate altogether. Changing the approach of a legacy system is not easy, because the contract demands might not be so simple. When you speak of legacy systems, you are inadvertently speaking of possible technical debts, outdated tech stacks, lack of architecture and modularity, data and process dependencies deeply ingrained into the system, and your workforce being comfortable around that system. All this and more results into an inertia that discourages people from moving to agile methods. What should you do in such cases? Well, move gradually, and decide when your team understands agile methods the same way they understood waterfall or the legacy method. Proper training and agile coaching should not be underestimated, and there's no need to specify the word agile too many times – it's a psychology I've noticed in people with traditional project management – the moment they hear of words like "agile," they panic. They'll probably end up mocking you and you might not like it. It's only simpler to make them think that you're going way and slowly, very slowly introduce the benefits of agile. Speaking of benefits, here is what the report says:

- Key benefits include **improved collaboration** (59%, around 465 respondents), better **alignment with business needs** (57%, roughly 449 people), and improved **software quality** (25%, about 197 respondents) (p. 13).

Improved collaboration is something I'd like to highlight. I recently heard of a situation, where an extremely capable manager, a stellar developer on Android, and a gem in backend development, all of whom I had personally worked with, got into a messy fight over another project that was easy to deliver. I delved a little deeper, and I found blame games. Still deeper and I found that there were no retros. Another deep dive and I found that there was no balanced documentation and the cognitive workload we spoke of in Chapter 5 was not taken into account by the senior leadership. What was all this, I thought? These people delivered happily with me. How could such a disaster happen? And they could speak callously of each other. Was it lack of agility? Did they know the meaning of agile? To begin with, I found my answers in the state of agile report cited above. Nothing can be as understated as team collaboration. A survey I did, for understanding Scrum, with a group of 50 leaders, gave me the same results. We discuss that survey in the next section. For now, it's just enough to know that if you only **understand** each other, you'll execute well.

Forty-four percent of respondents (around 346 people) highlighted the need for **end-to-end visibility**, while **34%** (about 268 respondents) emphasized the importance of measuring **cycle and wait times** to improve Agile's contribution to DevOps (p. 22, l. 44-34). This indicates that many organizations struggle with transparency and traceability, particularly from the business initiative stage through development, testing, and deployment. Again, increasing visibility is part of collaboration.

The significant focus on both visibility and metrics highlights that many organizations see Agile as a key driver for improving DevOps practices. It reflects a growing awareness that better measurement and visibility are foundational to achieving continuous integration, delivery, and deployment goals within a DevOps framework.

By now, if you did get to download the report, you'll see that agile is adopted by many sectors. Here's the download in brief:

- Just over 25% said their organizations were in the tech sector, while 17% were in financial services, and 7% were in healthcare/pharma, professional services, and government (p. 23).

My point here is that don't shirk because of the percentages in your sector – try it out and then reject it or accept it. Make sure you know the reasons why you want to shift to agile, and you'll not go wrong. The reasons will come from the ones we discussed in the evolution of agile and not just the buzz around it.

Summary

In this chapter, we touched topics that need books of their own. CAS, human-centric Agile, and agility as a habit – all these have well-written books. Their links are provided in the section "Further Reading." We also spoke of the main reason for this chapter – tapping the agility within and recognizing that all life forms are agile. We hope that our endeavor leaves a message for a holistic change and not just professional thinking. Here's to a more conscious society and a better world. That's all we need.

Further Reading

https://link.springer.com/chapter/10.1007/978-3-030-20309-2_1

https://link.springer.com/referenceworkentry/10.1007/
978-3-319-69909-7_104659-1

Index

A

ABCXYZ Corp
  communication blast, 112, 113
  component-based team
    structure, 109, 110
  problem identification
    combine Product Owner and
    Scrum Master, 119, 120
    component team structure,
    typical Org Chart, 122
    context switching, 117, 118
    feature-based teams, 123
    feature-based *vs.*
      component-based
      teams, 125
    lack of demos, 120
    lack of retrospectives, 121
    lean thinking, 115, 116
    reporting *vs.* delivery,
      118, 119
    team structure
      choice, 122–125
  Product Owner and the Scrum
    Master, 109
  project perspective,
    component-based team
    structure, 111
  reporting, 113

  Scrum, 109
  Scrum Masters, 109, 114
  three-fold solution
    Agile Manifesto, 125
    Conway's Law, 130–135
    lean thinking, 126
    retrospective
      philosophy, 127–130
    Scrum Guide, 127
    Unix, case study, 136, 137
  timesheet management, 114
Accountability matrix, 35
ACS, *see* Automated Case
    Support (ACS)
Actors and team structures
  accountability matrices, 106
  CAS, 106
  frameworks, 106
  team sizes, 107–109
Adaptation and transparency, 28
Administrative tasks, 92, 94, 95, 103
Affiliative leadership, 182
Agile, 201
  coaches (*see* Agile coaches)
  contract, 189, 190, 197
  human beings, 3
  mindset, 1, 2, 4
  social change, 201

© Kanika Sud 2025
K. Sud, *Customizable Agile Development*, https://doi.org/10.1007/979-8-8688-1055-8

Printed in the United States
by Baker & Taylor Publisher Services